STEVEN N. PESKIND

One Hundred Days Before Trial

A Family Lawyer's Guide to Preparation and Strategy

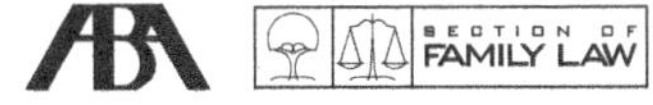

Cover by Amanda Fry/ABA Publishing.

Printed in the United States of America.

25 24 7 6

Library of Congress Cataloging-in-Publication Data

Names: Peskind, Steven N., author.
Title: One hundred days before trial : a family lawyer's guide to preparation and strategy first edition / by Steven N. Peskind.
Description: Chicago : American Bar Association, 2015. | Includes bibliographical references and index.
Identifiers: LCCN 2015041310 | ISBN 9781634253383 (print : alk. paper)
Subjects: LCSH: Matrimonial actions—United States. | Domestic relations courts—United States. | Pre-trial procedure—United States.
Classification: LCC KF505.5 .P47 2015 | DDC 346.7301/50269—dc23
LC record available at http://lccn.loc.gov/2015041310

Discounts are available for books ordered in bulk. Special consideration is given to state bars, CLE programs, and other bar-related organizations. Inquire at ABA Publishing, American Bar Association, 321 North Clark Street, Chicago, Illinois 60654-7598.

www.ShopABA.org

Dedication

To Barbara Morris Peskind, who prepared me.

Table of Contents

About the Author

Steven Peskind is the principal of the Peskind Law Firm based in St. Charles, Illinois. His firm concentrates in family law matters throughout the state of Illinois.

He graduated from Tulane University and DePaul College of Law. He is a fellow of the American Academy of Matrimonial Lawyers and is an elected member of the American Law Institute and the American Bar Foundation. He recently served on the Illinois Family Law Study Committee working to improve Illinois family laws.

Mr. Peskind is a faculty member of the Family Law Trial Advocacy Institute presented annually in Boulder, Colorado, by the ABA Family Law Section in conjunction with the National Institute of Trial Advocacy. In addition, he serves as co-chair of the Publication Board of the ABA Family Law Section. Mr. Peskind also serves on the faculty of the Oklahoma State Bar Family Law Section Trial Institute.

Mr. Peskind speaks nationally on a variety of family law topics. He has been the keynote speaker for several state family law presentations and has spoken on such diverse topics as evidence, trial techniques, practice management, and the future of family law practice.

Prior to this publication, Mr. Peskind had written three books. *The Family Law Trial Evidence Handbook* was published by the ABA in 2013. In 2014, Mr. Peskind wrote *Divorce In Illinois*, published by Addicus Press. In 2015, he published *The Changing Face of Illinois Family Law: 2016 Marriage and Dissolution of Marriage Act Overhaul* through the Illinois Institute of Continuing Legal Education. Mr. Peskind has also written numerous chapters and articles, including three law review articles. The law review articles examined redefining parentage in the age of assisted reproductive technology, the origin and utility of the best interest standard in determining child custody, and hearsay evidence in child custody proceedings. In 2005 he was inducted into Scribes, a legal writing honor society.

Mr. Peskind has been recognized as one of the Best Lawyers in America. The Leading Lawyers Network has designated Mr. Peskind a Leading Lawyer since 2003 and the *Super Lawyers* has recognized him as a Super Lawyer since 2008. In 2015, Best Lawyers honored him with the award of Family Lawyer of the Year in Chicago.

Foreword

In the mid-summer of 2012 I received a telephone call from a respected colleague, inviting me at nearly the last minute to participate as a faculty member at the American Bar Association's annual Family Law Trial Advocacy Institute. The Institute is presented every summer in partnership with the National Institute for Trial Advocacy in Boulder, Colorado. I was thrilled and terrified—thrilled to receive the invitation to participate as a faculty member for such a valuable course in the field of family law, and terrified I would be asked to help teach a subject to others that I still find challenging after 30 years as a lawyer: trial practice and the substantive law of evidence. Nevertheless, I was game to try.

Upon my arrival that first summer, I was immediately impressed by the soft-spoken lawyer on the faculty who taught evidence and trial advocacy with precision, confidence, and the simple eloquence possessed by true experts. Steven Peskind, a graduate of the Institute and a regular member of its faculty for many years, has long made evidence and trial practice key focuses of his scholarly interests (along with tai chi, yoga, spirituality, the life and writings of Abraham Lincoln, and a diverse variety of other pursuits). He presents complex subject matter in a way that makes it seem perfectly understandable, rational, and logical. I was excited to learn that he had just written a book for the ABA Family Law Section, entitled *The Family Law Trial Evidence Handbook*. His approach was so compelling that I immediately acquired this treatise, which quickly became the most important practical book in my law library. Now, with *One Hundred Days Before Trial*, Steven addresses the *pretrial* phase of family law cases, articulating a disciplined, flexible, and effective approach to the enormous task of trial preparation.

One of my lawyer friends often jokes that, no matter how well prepared, "there is not a trial lawyer alive who doesn't round the corner to the courthouse on the morning of trial, secretly hoping to find it is surrounded by fire engines and has a 'closed for the day' sign prominently displayed!" There is a great deal of truth to this remark. Why is this so? I think it is true, at least in part, because of the tremendous responsibility assumed by lawyers who advocate for clients with real-world, day-to-day problems involving that which is most important to every individual: the future of one's immediate family. This is hard work! The expectations are substantial. Each of us in marital and family law feels this responsibility daily, and it becomes all the more acute as a trial approaches and we attempt to distill mountains of detailed information into a persuasive, thematic package. Our clients are not corporations, institutions, or insurance companies with litigation budgets, general counsel, and sophisticated litigation experience upon which to draw for guidance and assurance. Our clients are individual human beings, most of whom have never stepped into a courthouse, and whose quality of life and family fortunes are on the line. They look to us for guidance and assurance. Developing methods of practice allowing us to effectively carry this burden for the client in a way that we, too, can maintain a healthy life, is a central pursuit for any trial lawyer.

Steven's latest book embraces this challenge. *One Hundred Days Before Trial* focuses on creating a persuasive vision of the case prior to trial, and developing the necessary internal systems ensuring proper and thorough preparation—systems applicable to all cases, which allow us to carry this load of interests and expectations with confidence and skill, and with the assurance that our clients receive our very best and most effective efforts in every case. Steven's book outlines an approach to trial preparation and practice that has worked successfully for the finest family law attorneys in our profession for years.

In a previous book, Steven wrote that "[n]ot every case can be concluded at the conference table. Even in this era of ADR, complete family lawyers still need the skills to resolve their cases in court." If this is true (and I believe it is), gifted and experienced trial lawyers are harder to find than ever before. That is why books such as this one are so important to our profession. I am certain the reader will find it as instructive as I have.

When Steven asked me to write the foreword to this book, I was again both thrilled and terrified. I was thrilled to have the honor of writing this foreword for such an excellent manual for trial preparation for all marital and family law attorneys, and I was terrified that I would not be able to do justice either to the book or its author in the brief pages I was invited to write. It really doesn't matter. *One Hundred Days Before Trial*, like *The Family Law Trial Evidence Handbook* before it, is a practical and useful resource for the family trial lawyer. You will be glad you own this book, and you will be a more effective trial lawyer because you do.

Cary J. Mogerman, Esq.

Introduction

Yes, there's such a thing as luck in trial work but it only comes at 3:00 o'clock in the morning. . . . You'll find me in the library looking for luck at 3:00 o'clock in the morning.

—Louis Nizer

This book is a guideline to help family lawyers overcome their fear of the courtroom—it provides an antidote to trial anxiety, usually caused by poor planning and insecurity. I offer an alternative to the mad-dash scramble model of trial preparation. My message is simple: start early with the end in mind, develop a plan, and maintain self-discipline to work the plan on a regular basis.

Advance planning empowers you and enhances your ability to represent clients. But more than improving trial performance, systematic planning produces better settlements and a better quality of life. If well prepared, you can earn respect from your peers, increasing the likelihood of compromise: other lawyers are much more likely to settle cases when they know you can try a case. And when well prepared, you can settle a case for the right reasons rather than collapsing because of poor planning or self-doubt.

While trials are inherently fluid and often unpredictable, lawyers can manage self-doubt by embracing the turbulence. If lawyers are prepared and mindful, they can adapt and overcome. Preparation increases confidence and thus performance; well-prepared lawyers are more relaxed and natural, improving their credibility and persuasiveness. The well-prepared lawyer can concentrate on telling the client's story, rather than worrying about where the next exhibit might be located.

What skills must an effective trial lawyer have? First, lawyers must possess a working knowledge of the rule of evidence, the language of the courtroom. They must also study the art of advocacy:

how to package evidence in the most persuasive manner. Reduced to its essence, preparing for trial is not complicated. Which facts are necessary to support your theory and advance the theme of the case? Will expert witnesses be necessary to prove any elements of the theory? What other witnesses can contribute to telling the story? What documents will support or confirm the theory? How should you plan for adverse evidence? Trying a divorce case is not placing a man on the moon—it just requires advance thought and planning. They say the thousand-mile journey starts with one step, and indeed a trial is the lawyer's thousand-mile journey.

In the hurly-burly of modern practice, it's hard to find the time (or self-discipline) for early trial planning, but you must dedicate yourself. Success rarely results from last-minute preparation—in fact, calamities often occur. To achieve peace of mind, you must think ahead, plan better, and "arrive at the battle early." It is my hope that this book will give you the tools to help your clients and also yourself.

This book is broken into segments based upon arbitrary time periods. The reader need not precisely follow the schedules suggested; they are simply guidelines to consider. Each case is different, and you must prepare according to each case's dynamics. What is essential and common to all cases, however, is the necessity to think first, act second, and be mindful throughout of both the big picture and the fine details.

When your trial date is set, I advocate beginning with the end: determining through visualization and creative exercises the desired result to be achieved. Next, I provide a framework to help you accumulate the facts and thoughts on how to package them for an effective and persuasive trial. From there, I suggest ideas for organizing the case: how to prepare your exhibits, examinations, and witnesses. I continue by showing you how to bring it all together: how to take your work product and translate it into a trial presentation. I offer suggestions on how to spend the last week before the commencement of the trial and conclude with tips for wrapping things up after the trial.

The idea for this book originated with the ABA family law section CLE committee that developed this topic for a seminar at its fall 2013 CLE conference in Deer Valley, Utah. I would also like to recognize my co-presenters Chris Melcher and Richard Ferguson for stimulating me to write on this topic. Many of the ideas in this book are derived from that presentation. Also, I would like to recognize the brilliant faculty and students of the ABA Family Law Trial Advocacy Institute presented by the ABA Family Law Section and the National Institute of Trial Advocacy. This program has made me a better lawyer and continues to influence many of my thoughts about trial advocacy. I am humbled by the opportunity to spend a week each year with such talented lawyers.

I would also like to thank the ABA Family Law Section Publication Board. In particular, I would like to thank my mentors Gail Baker and Linda Ravdin for inspiring me to write books for the ABA. Linda served as my lay editor for both this book and *The Family Law Evidence Handbook*, and her comments and suggestions have materially improved the final product. I would also like to thank Jeff Salyards, my professional editor, for his friendship and guidance. Jeff has provided invaluable help and support for this book.

Due to this book's focus, I will not be addressing trial techniques in any detail. To the extent that those techniques influence methods of preparing, I will tangentially discuss them. There are many exceptional books written on trial advocacy, and many of them were used as resources for this book. For a list of these resources, please review the bibliography at the end of this book.

The chapters will be broken down, with the assumption that a trial date has been set roughly 100 days out. Obviously, this is not always the case, but the principles discussed can be applied regardless; the key is to think about the desired outcome and the tasks necessary to achieve it.

Section of Family Law Publications Development Board

CHAPTER 1
100 Days Before Trial

I have watched the reflection of the rising sun on my computer screen many a morning while my opponents have slept their lives away peacefully, so peacefully.

—Gerry Spence

Introduction

When the trial date is set, first script the trial in your mind. Determine the legal theory: the skeleton of the case. Also identify the beating heart of the case—the reason why your position is the right one for the judge to embrace. Think of trial preparation as a giant jigsaw puzzle that includes documents, witnesses, the law, and procedure. Use your imagination. Visualize the scene depicted in the puzzle and collect all of the pieces. By seeing the case unfold in your mind first, you can prepare for the actual trial in an efficient, focused, and productive manner.

Master the Facts of Your Case

Edward Bennett Williams captured the essence of trial work: "There is no substitute for knowing everything." When your trial date is set, read your entire client file. Read the pleadings, documents produced, deposition transcripts or notes, subpoena replies, research memos, and any other information in your case file. This exercise, while mundane, gives you both a context for the case and will help germinate the impressions, theories, and themes you will use to prepare for trial.

Much of the early preparation is mental, and the impressions that are obtained from a simple reading of the case file will help guide both the preparation and the presentation of the case. In your trial journal (discussed on page 5), write down reminders to yourself, tasks to complete, thoughts, and general annotations prompted by your review of the case file.

Study the Law

Despite all of the swirling emotions in a family law case, never lose sight that it is a legal proceeding. Know the law and procedure. When entering a new case, the great trial lawyer David Boies gathers all of the important decisions related to the case and rereads them—and so should you. Due to our familiarity with our statutes and important cases in our jurisdiction, we assume we know the law and don't bother researching unless it becomes absolutely necessary. This is a mistake. The law is the foundation: the place where we should start. Read the applicable statute and the commentary. Look at its history and how it has evolved. Read the pertinent case law and see if you can determine any trends from the recent decisions. Find secondary authorities that comment on the particular issues. The law offers many opportunities for persuasion if you just make the time to study it.

Prepare an Outcome Narrative

After the trial date is scheduled, and you have reviewed your file and the pertinent law, start preparing by thinking about the *end* of the case. A focus on the end of the case will guide the preparation. By the time that trial is set, most of the discovery and investigation should be complete and the issues well defined. Hopefully, by now you have ascertained and clarified your client's specific goals. That is your target, and all aspects of preparation should point to that objective. Always keep the goals and outcomes in mind. A focused approach to the case prioritizes and streamlines preparation and also helps evaluate any future settlement offers.

Write down the specific outcome to make it concrete. Unlike the more detailed proposed findings and orders discussed later in this chapter, the outcome narrative is a short reminder of your ultimate goals for the case. Summarize the exact result you are seeking on behalf of your client. For example:

> James Martin is awarded primary residential custody of Sally and Tommy Martin. He is awarded alimony from Angelica Martin in the amount of $10,000 per month. He is awarded as his separate property the marital residence.

Write your outcome statement in the present tense. Goal setting experts advocate making your goals affirmatively, as though they have already happened. As success coach Tony Robbins states, "Setting goals is the first step in turning the invisible into the visible." By writing your goals, your brain will subconsciously develop strategies to help you achieve the desired result. Learn to harness the power of your subconscious as well as your conscious mind.

This exercise serves two purposes. First, it will serve as the first page of your trial notebook, keeping the desired result in the front of your mind throughout both the preparation and trial of the case. Second, it serves as the starting point for the preparation of the proof chart, which will be discussed later in this chapter.

Prepare a Case Notebook

Once you have read the case file and studied the law, if you have not done so earlier, prepare a case notebook. This notebook will evolve into the trial notebook. The case notebook is different from the client file containing the pleadings, orders, correspondence, etc. The case notebook is a resource to assist you in both planning and analysis of the issues in the case. Creation and maintenance of a case notebook allows you to quickly and easily access important information during trial preparation. Using the case notebook throughout the planning process is just as important as using one to keep you organized at the trial itself. Use the notebook to retain thoughts and ideas about the case.

Development of the Case Notebook

The case notebook must be prepared well before trial, but how early should you prepare it? Each case is different; the level of complexity and issues vary, and the creation of the notebook will depend on those variables. Notebooks started earlier in the case will evolve over time. Again, the key is functionality. Use your notebook as a practical resource to help keep everything organized and as a quick reference.

Create a notebook for each case that is not likely to quickly or easily settle. High-conflict cases are ideal candidates for the early creation of such a notebook. The preliminary notebook can be physical, digital, or a combination of both. While I use a three-ring notebook at trial, the early version of the notebook is digital: an Evernote notebook.[1] Evernote allows the creation of a digital notebook with subfiles in each individual notebook. Whether the choice is digital or analog, the concept is the same: save important information to the case notebook as a reference and aid for trial preparation or settlement negotiations.

In terms of the preliminary notebook's structure, use various subfolders for the individual case, categorizing important data. While each case is unique, consider the following subfolders:

1. **Outcome narrative**. What are our goals? What are we trying to achieve in this case?
2. **Proofs**. This is the folder where you will keep your proof chart.[2] Within this folder, list the important facts that you need to prove at the trial. If the proof chart is supplemented periodically as the case evolves, it saves much preparation time toward the end. As the case progresses and you discover information that you will likely need as evidence, log it in this folder. Always be mindful of events as they occur in the case: Is this something I may want to use as evidence at trial?
3. **Exhibits**. As discovery proceeds and documents are exchanged, consider which documents you may ultimately use as exhibits. In this folder, keep an inventory of those documents. If you maintain a paperless office, copy important documents that may serve as potential exhibits to a discrete digital "exhibit" folder. Alternatively, if you are not paperless, keep a log of potential exhibits or copy them to a physical exhibit folder.

1. Evernote is a Web-based application that can be found at http://www.evernote.com.

2. See page 15 for a discussion of proof charts.

4. **Law**. As you read new cases or developments that affect your case, save them here for reference as you prepare for trial. Any memoranda that you or your team prepares concerning the issues in the case should be saved here as well.
5. **Evidentiary issues**. As you think about your proofs and exhibits, are there any special challenges? Use this folder as a journal to log any concerns or thoughts about the admissibility of the evidence. Insert any cases or references that you will need to rely on.
6. **Themes**. Here, note any themes that occur to you as you work up the case. Always think of the emotional pull of the case. Think of ways to encapsulate that aspect of the statement into a simple statement. Keep your notes regarding all thoughts, impressions, and ideas that you have regarding the heart of your case, the aspects of the case that will appeal to the judge emotionally.
7. **Journal**. Use your journal as a mind dump regarding the case. In the journal, record any random thoughts or comments, anything that you might want to refer to later.
8. **Checklist**. Use of a trial preparation checklist will help focus your preparation. Use a trial preparation checklist throughout the pretrial stages of the case to make sure everything necessary is accomplished. See the comprehensive trial preparation checklist in the appendix.
9. **Witnesses**. Keep a list of potential witnesses and the purpose for their testimony. Witnesses serve two important purposes: the witness may provide testimony concerning a fact probative of an issue in the case, but the witness may also be called to lay the foundation for an exhibit. In either case, indicate in your notes whether the witnesses will be easily available, cooperative, and subject to service of a subpoena.

Update the Notebook Regularly

Set aside time regularly to review the case's progress and update your notebook as necessary. Always keep your eyes fixed on the horizon: where does the information you are accumulating fit into the jigsaw puzzle? Having a central depository for important case information saves time and your sanity.

Think Your Way to a Successful Result

Trial preparation must begin in the lawyer's mind. Thinking through the issues, strategies, and ultimate goals of the client requires disciplined and dedicated time just for thinking. As lawyers, we are prone toward action. But before we build the building, we need to design it in our heads. As trial lawyer Lloyd Paul Stryker noted in his trial advocacy treatise, *The Art of Advocacy*:

> By thinking, imagination will be whetted and from thinking and imagination, ideas will spring and those ideas may become the key to a successful verdict. By thinking you will evolve the strategy and tactics of your case, and a campaign in the courtroom is as dependent upon strategy and tactics as on the field of battle.[3]

Theory

The case theory is the skeletal outline of the legal issues in the case. What is the legal basis for the desired relief? In other words, what legal elements underlie the claim? Often in a matrimonial case there are several legal theories supporting financial or child custody claims. There may be alternate theories supporting the desired relief. The lawyer must decide on the most persuasive way to package the theory because the evidence and arguments flow from it. James W. McElhaney described a case theory in his book:

> The theory of the case is the basic underlying idea that explains not only the legal theory and factual background, but also ties as much of the evidence as possible into a coherent and credible whole. Whether it is simple and unadorned or subtle and sophisticated, the theory of the case is a product of the advocate. It is the basic concept around which everything else revolves.[4]

Theories derive from legal principles. For example, why is your client legally entitled to spousal support? Identify the statutory or

---

3. Lloyd Paul Stryker, The Art of Advocacy 26 (1954).
4. James W. McElhaney, McElhaney's Trial Notebook 78 (3d ed. 1998).

common-law factors supporting the claim and write out your theory as a narrative to help you focus:

> Jane Smith sacrificed her career and the ability to support herself in order to promote John Smith's career and care for the family. John should be required to assist her to maintain the marital standard of living as a result of this sacrifice.

Another way of looking at this is as a syllogistic exercise. Identify the issue and the underlying requirements to support the desired result. For example:

> 750 ILCS 5/504 of the Illinois Marriage and Dissolution of Marriage Act permits a court to award maintenance for long-term marriages where a spouse supported the other spouse's career, contributed as a homemaker to the family, and as a result lost opportunity for personal professional achievement. Here the parties were married 12 years; Jane Smith relocated twice as a result of John Smith's job transfers, and accordingly gave up her career. Jane Smith is entitled to maintenance.

Write down the theories of the case and use them as your index throughout all aspects of trial preparation.

Themes

Trying a case boils down to telling a coherent story that moves the judge to act in your client's favor. To do so, you need to develop a theme for your case. The theme encapsulates the emotional pull of the case: the reason why the relief you are seeking is the right thing for the judge to do. Good themes are memorable, pertinent, and resonate with the judge. Like a musical score that appears at critical times throughout a film, a trial theme appears periodically during the trial to help the judge remember the heart of the case.

Ideally, a theme should fit all aspects of the case, which is difficult to do in a case that has issues as varied as child custody and the valuation and division of a family business. Do your best to see if any all-encompassing theme is available, and if not, use different themes for different aspects of the case. Try not to have more than two or three themes in any case.

Once you have chosen a theme, work to find a grabber, a short phrase that summarizes the theme. The grabber should be used at various intervals throughout the case. Start the opening with the grabber and circle back to it during the examinations and the closing. If the theme is a mother's constant sacrifice for her children, the grabber might be "She gave everything." Or if the theme is a father's stability, the grabber might be "Like a rock." Think of creative ways to paint a visual image of the theme and storyline in a few words.

Developing a powerful theme is critical; it anchors the judge with a reference that will make your case more memorable and accessible.

Visualization

With the theory, theme, and desired outcome developed, consider mentally trying the case. As Lloyd Paul Stryker observed, "Imagination for the trial lawyer is as essential as for the novelist, the artist or the poet." If one can tap into one's subconscious mind to help plan, many ideas will develop and come into focus. Positive visualization is a proven tool to help people achieve desired results.[5] Athletes regularly rely on visualization to enhance performance.[6] For example, Jack Nicklaus regularly used visualization: "I never hit a shot, not even in practice, without having a very sharp in-focus picture of it in my head."

Chinese philosophy incorporates a principle known as *wu wei*, roughly translated as "trying not to try." Effortless action results in positive outcomes. With this exercise, you can relax into the trial and allow your subconscious to script it for you. Relaxation enhances your creativity and ingenuity and allows you to visualize your trial. Keep an open mind; this exercise is a helpful tool to capture the essence of your case.

Find a quiet room and ensure no interruptions. Make sure to relax; if you can meditate for a few minutes in advance, that is a helpful warm-up. It is not necessary to have the file open on the desk, but keep a legal pad for notes. Start by imagining the courtroom and the

---

5. For more information on positive visualization, see Shakti Gawain, Creative Visualization: Use the Power of Your Imagination to Create What You Want in Your Life (2002).

6. Christopher Clarey, *Olympians Use Imagery as Mental Training*, N.Y. Times (Feb. 22, 2014), http://www.nytimes.com/2014/02/23/sports/olympics/olympians-use-imagery-as-mental-training.html?_r=0.

judge presiding. Visualize as much detail as possible to help simulate the reality of the exercise. Imagine the opponent across the room and both parties sitting at counsel table. What is everybody wearing? See the court clerk busily shuffling papers. Imagine the clerk or the judge calling the case and asking if everybody is ready to proceed.

Present your opening statement. Are you standing at a podium or sitting at counsel table? What is this case about? Identify your theme by presenting your grabber. Give the judge a road map of the issues and a context for the evidence. Does the structure of the opening naturally unfold in your mind? If so, write down a quick outline and any other notes related to it. Ask the judge for your requested relief at the end of your opening. Make it as real as possible.

What is your opponent saying in his or her opening statement? Is your opponent thematically responding to your opening or developing his or her own theme? What is the story of the opposing case?

Call your client as a witness. Walk through the relevant facts supporting your theory. Imagine your client actually responding to your questions. Is the client clear in his or her answers? Or are the answers disjointed and uncertain? Let your imagination guide the examination. Write down any revelations. As you work through your examination, note the sequence of your questions.

Visualize the opponent cross-examining your client. What topics is the opponent covering? Where does your client have exposure? How is your client responding under pressure? See your client as argumentative, or passive. Your subconscious will fill in the blanks. Write down notes to help you later prepare your client to withstand the adverse examination.

Imagine the opposing spouse testifying. Is the spouse confident or tentative? Let your subconscious play based upon your observations of the spouse throughout the case. Also, consider the comments you have heard from the opposing counsel throughout the case; these comments often foreshadow the type of testimony you will hear once the witnesses are sworn. Next, imagine your cross-examination of the opponent. Is there a particular factual issue in contention? If so, what areas will you explore during your adverse examination of the spouse? Write down things that pop into your head as you think through the cross-examination.

Are there any other witnesses? Apply this exercise to those witnesses as well, thinking through the areas that you and your opponent will likely explore during your respective examinations. Use this exercise to help you choose your witnesses as well. Again, jot down notes as you work through the examinations in order to reference them later when you are more formally preparing for the examinations.

Present your closing argument. Recount the evidence that was presented in a persuasive manner. What is the structure of the argument? Pay attention and make note if it is fluid and natural. Listen to the opponent's closing. What topics are the opposing counsel stressing? Where is the argument getting traction? Your subconscious mind is telegraphing where you will need to focus as you prepare your case.

The final step, and perhaps the most important, is to imagine the judge rendering a decision. Imagine the judge ruling in your client's favor on all of the various contested rulings. Will the judge rule from the bench or will you receive a written ruling? Feel the excitement as you notify your client that the court ruled in your client's favor and the client's grateful response. Note your emotions and the satisfaction you feel after receiving the positive result.

Mental practice, such as this one, helps focus the mind on the ultimate goal. The famous Russian dissident, Natan Sharansky, while imprisoned in solitary confinement in Russia, used visualization to master chess. He played chess matches in his mind, reasoning that with the time he had he could become a world-class chess player. After leaving prison, he ultimately defeated world champion Garry Kasparov.[7] World-class athletes and other competitive peak performers use this type of exercise, and lawyers can certainly benefit from the practice.

The Garner Approach

Legal-writing guru Bryan Garner suggests a four-step process to prepare for a writing project. The madman-architect-carpenter-judge system was developed by Dr. Betty Flowers, and it applies equally well to trial planning. Under this system, organization is broken into four phases:

1. **The Madman Phase**. In this phase, all ideas regarding the case are put on paper, randomly and indiscriminately. The madman simply lets loose with all possible thoughts that can later be synthesized and organized. These might include thoughts about

7. A.J. Levan, *Seeing Is Believing: The Power of Visualization*, PSYCHOL. TODAY (Dec. 2, 2009), http://www.psychologytoday.com/blog/flourish/200912/seeing-is-believing-the-power-visualization.

the theory and theme, witness testimony, exhibits, grabbers, and anything else that might be used at the trial. During this phase, all ideas are indiscriminately written down.

2. **The Architect Phase**. The architect takes the ideas generated by the madman and starts to connect them, ending with a linear outline of the entire trial. From the opening through the closing, the key aspects of the trial are outlined. Garner says, "The more detailed the architectural plans, the better."[8]
3. **The Carpenter Phase**. Working off the architectural plans, the carpenter creates all of the structures based upon the architect's specs. The carpenter drafts the opening statement, direct examination, cross topics, and closing. According to Garner, the carpenter must "write rapidly, without editing along the way, simply filling in the details according to the architectural specs."[9]
4. **The Judge Phase**. During this final phase, the judge takes the completed components and edits them. Note that during the earlier phases, the focus was on creativity and generation of ideas. During this final phase, the focus is on troubleshooting and critical thinking. Troubleshoot your work product for potential snares, corniness, overplaying arguments, and any other problems with the general presentation.

Using this approach to organizing, you can break your preparation into discrete steps, which makes an apparently overwhelming task more manageable.

Mind Mapping

As another creative exercise, consider mind mapping. Mind mapping is a method of accessing intelligence and enhancing creativity. Use mind mapping to help you think visually about trial, prompting your subconscious to connect the issues and the supporting evidence.

Wikipedia defines a mind map as

> a diagram used to visually organize information. A mind map is often created around a single concept, drawn as an image in the center of a blank landscape page, to which associated representations of ideas such as images, words and parts of words are added.

8. Bryan A. Garner, The Winning Brief 5 (2d ed. 2004).
9. *Id.*

Major ideas are connected directly to the central concept, and other ideas branch out from those.[10]

The creator of this concept, Tony Buzan, defines it as a "powerful graphic technique, which provides a universal key to unlocking the potential of the brain. The Mind Map can be applied to every aspect of life where improved learning and clearer thinking will enhance human performance."[11] According to Buzan, a mind map consists of four essential characteristics:

1. The subject of attention is crystallized in a central image.
2. The main themes of the subject radiate from the central image as branches.
3. Branches consist of a key image or word printed on an associated line. Topics of lesser importance are also represented as branches attached to higher-level branches.
4. The branches form a connected nodal structure.[12]

Mind mapping can be done with pen and paper, using multicolored pens for emphasis. Or there are various mind-mapping software applications that can be used for the same purpose. Here is an example of a mind map for a relocation hearing:

FIGURE 1

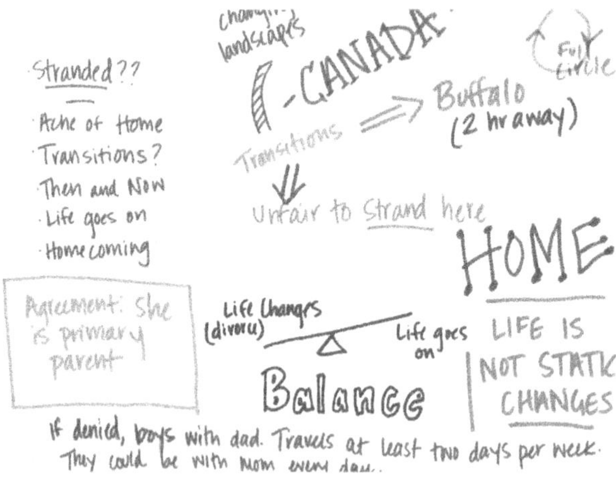

10. *Mind Map*, Wikipedia, http://en.wikipedia.org/wiki/Mind_map (last updated July 13, 2015).

11. Tony Buzan & Barry Buzan, The Mind Map Book 59 (1996).

12. *Id.*

Use the mind-mapping exercise as a visual way to illustrate the theories, themes, proofs, and any other meaningful information you might use in the presentation of the case.

Think!

The foregoing creativity exercises help you think about the elements of your case in anticipation of the trial. These exercises can be used for any other aspect of the case as well: preparing for a deposition, an important meeting, or a contested hearing. Of course, you are not limited to these techniques; they are merely suggested models to help provoke thought.

The key to effective preparation is to stimulate thinking, which is the essence of trial preparation—taking the discordant parts of a case and tying them together in the most persuasive manner. Once the reflection exercises are complete, the next step is to determine how best to organize the various ideas. While there is no right way of harnessing the information, what is important is having a target to aim for. One manner of doing this is to start at the end of the case with a proposed judgment supported by findings.

Prepare a Final Judgment

Prepare a judgment containing all of the relief you are seeking in the case. Assume the court grants your client's wish list. What would be contained in the ruling? And from there, consider the facts the judge needs to find in order to support such a ruling. For example, assume your client is seeking an award of alimony in the amount of $8,000 per month. Draft your proposed judgment to reflect that award. Next, focus on the findings that the court would need to make to support the award. Consult the statute and case law and consider the elements that one needs to prove to sustain the alimony award. Plug in the facts of your case into your findings:

1. The Court orders John Jones to pay Ellen Jones the sum of $8,000 per month for spousal support.
2. The Court finds the following:
   a. Ellen Jones has insufficient resources to maintain her lifestyle based upon the former marital standard of living.

b. John Jones earns a gross annual income of $350,000 per year; he has sufficient resources to contribute toward Ellen's support.
c. Ellen contributed toward John's professional success in the following manner:
   i. Ellen's full-time care for the children allowed John to pursue professional opportunities.
   ii. Ellen's availability for the children allowed John the freedom to travel, which led to the advancement of his career.
   iii. Ellen regularly accompanied John to work social events and entertained his coworkers at the parties' home.
d. Ellen is unemployed as a result of providing homemaker services to the family.
e. Ellen has limited employment opportunities as a result of her domestic responsibilities, her age, and lack of work experience.

This exercise allows you to focus on the necessary evidence to support such a result. Use this exercise for all aspects of the case: property division, child custody, asset classification, etc. Not only does it provide a road map for the necessary evidence, it also can be used at the conclusion of the case as an outline for the closing argument and can (after revisions to make it consistent with the actual evidence) be presented to the court as your proposed findings and requested relief. If it is submitted digitally in a format that allows the judge to alter it as necessary, it assists the judge in preparing his or her own judgment (using your template to do so!).[13]

Anticipate Your Opponent's Case

During your process of visualizing your case, spend time thinking about your opponent's case. Review your opponent's pleadings and

---

13. Consider submitting proposed orders to the court whenever possible. Even in motion practice, proposed orders help both the lawyer and the court. By preparing such an order, the advocate clarifies the specific relief that he is seeking on behalf of the client. The judge benefits because the order gets to the heart of the requested relief in a written format that is easy to follow. And often, when a judge is rushed (as often happens in a high-volume court call), the judge may be more inclined to grant the relief in the preprinted court order that is ready to sign.

other documents that may predict his or her ultimate theory or theme. Consider how you would approach the case if you represented the opposing party. How would you argue the case? Hopefully you were paying attention when the opposing lawyer repeatedly tried his case to you in the courthouse hallway. Read your client's deposition transcript to see what type of issues the opposing lawyer focused on. Prepare a summary of the key points that you will need to refute as part of your case.

Prepare a Proof Chart

The final step in the preliminary planning process is to determine and organize your proofs. Proofs are simply those facts necessary to prove the theory of the case. And it is facts that win cases. A proof chart is a visual summary that helps a trial lawyer consider and organize those proofs. It is also a template to help you think about any evidentiary obstacles in advance. Use the chart to organize the proofs in a coherent and strategic way for the most persuasive presentation possible. Here is an example of such a chart:

TABLE 1

Fact	Issue	How to Prove	Foundation/ Authentication	Objections and Responses
Ellen is a stay-at-home mom	Alimony/ property division	Ellen testify	N/A	None
John's salary $500K per year	Alimony/ property	Employer records	Fed. R. E. 902 (11) certification?	Hearsay? Business record?

The fact section is obvious: What fact do you need to prove to support the theory of the case? What issue or issues does this fact support? Often facts support multiple issues.

Next, consider the best way to prove the necessary fact. There are five ways to prove any particular fact: (1) witness testimony, (2) a document or object (e.g., photograph), (3) stipulation, (4) admission, or (5) judicial notice. Consider the competing interests of efficiency and emotion. For example, one could seek a stipulation that Ellen is a homemaker. But what would impact your judge more: a dry recitation of fact in a written stipulation or Ellen testifying to the grind of her typical day, chauffeuring the kids in six different directions along with all of her other assorted daily responsibilities? As Gerry Spence observed: "Judges are said to make their decisions in accordance with the logic of the law. But I say that good judges like the rest of us, make their decisions from their heart zone first, after which they support their decisions with logic."[14] Weigh this when considering how best to present your case.

Don't address just the positive facts you need to prove but also the facts you will need to address in response to problems with your case. Don't overlook your negatives. What evidence do you need to explain away negative conduct? What makeup do you need for your blemishes? Make a list of all of the positive facts of your case as well as the negatives.

In developing your theme and theory, your focus is more on the abstract. In developing the proof chart, the focus shifts to the concrete. Cite specific examples of conduct, tangible images that you can connect to your theory and theme. Use sensory details as part of the proofs. Trial lawyer Michael Tigar observes that judges and jurors

> bring all their faculties in making sense of a case: intuition, feeling, and attitude, as well as the ostensibly rational process of inductive and deductive reasoning. Therefore, persuasion through evidence must reach all of these faculties. We are returning to the historic roots of rhetoric, and we are seeing the unity of rhetoric and theatre.[15]

Thus, when completing the proof chart, consider not only what to get into evidence but also the best way to do so. Remember: both show and tell whenever possible. Appeal to the judge's heart as well as the judge's intellect. Think of interesting and creative ways to tell your client's story that will keep the judge's attention. Remember, your judge has probably heard similar facts hundreds if not thousands of times before. You need to think of a fresh way to present these facts to engage the judge.

---

14. Gerry Spence, How to Argue and Win Every Time 188 (1995).
15. Michael E. Tigar, Examining Witnesses 30 (2d ed. 2003).

Be careful when preparing proofs not to simply throw things at the judge. Quantity of evidence rarely outweighs quality. If a judge is inundated with unnecessary records or redundant testimony, the impact of the important evidence will be lost. Use only what you need, neither less nor more. Sometimes unprepared lawyers take a bushel barrel approach to evidence, admitting reams of paper to try to add weight or gravity to the case. But as skilled trial lawyers know, trials are not won based upon the number of banker's boxes hauled into court each day. As Edward Bennett Williams observed, "A measure of a great trial lawyer is what the lawyer leaves in his briefcase."

Your proof chart will evolve over time, as the preparation unfolds. But the starting point needs to be to get it down on paper. For months you have been carrying around various facts and ideas in your head. Clear all of those details by getting them down on paper. Besides helping as a guide to trial preparation, this exercise is psychologically refreshing. The act of purging onto paper will give you a sense of relief and control.

Organize Your Team

Who are the people that will assist you in your journey? Unless you are a solo practitioner who works alone, you will rely on the help of others to get ready. The team may be as small as one assistant or include multiple associates and paralegals. Consider your expert and consultant team members as well. Think about the human resources available and their respective roles in helping you to prepare. Have an organizational meeting to discuss the issues and brainstorm the general direction of the case. Identify everybody's role and the types of tasks that the team members will assume responsibility for. At the organizational meeting, schedule follow-up meetings and block the time out now, and consider your follow-up meetings inviolate. While the complexity of the issues dictate how frequently the team should meet, the following schedule is a sensible timetable to consider: 90 days, 60 days, 45 days, 30 days, and weekly thereafter.

Depending on the complexity of the case, consider using an associate and/or a paralegal at the trial itself. In that event, advise those team members that you are considering using them at the trial so they can plan ahead and there are no scheduling conflicts. These team members are integral to the planning process and should be involved in all meetings if possible. Use your team to brainstorm, plan, and generally to assist you to achieve a positive result for your client.

Protect Your Calendar

Lawyer's calendars fill up quickly. Set aside preparation time *now* to avoid having to cram the weekend before the trial. Block out time in your calendar today and protect it like a mother bear protecting her cub. Stay disciplined. Urgent matters undoubtedly will arise, and if you don't protect the sanctity of your preparation time slots, they will continuously be pushed back and may jeopardize your entire case. If the reserved time slots are used for other tasks under the mistaken assumption that "I have plenty of time to prepare, the trial isn't for a month," you will undoubtedly regret it. That month will come before you know it. Discuss with your assistant the need to protect your preparation time and seek his or her help to keep you on track. Make your assistant the jealous guard of your calendar and direct him or her to insist that you honor your commitment to yourself.

Depending upon the complexity of the case, set aside one hour per week to review the status of your case workup and prepare materials or examinations. Use this as hard-thinking time and don't multitask. Sometimes it is helpful to leave the office to have quiet concentration time. Review your trial journal or checklist and use reminders to monitor team members or yourself. No project is too big if you break it into small manageable tasks and follow through on them on a regular basis.

Discuss Fees

Discuss fees with your client at the onset of trial preparation. Give the client an honest idea both of the likely fees and costs and your expectations regarding payment. Develop a plan to make sure you are paid before rather than after the trial. Many clients are more likely to pay for hope today rather than out of gratitude later. It is not uncommon for someone to turn his or her back on the well after the thirst is satisfied. If you have an existing balance at this point, it will only grow over the coming months, and unless concrete plans are in place early, your focus will be moved from your client's issues to your own lack of compensation. Consider an evergreen retainer plan for trial work, placing a sum into trust and having the client pay monthly until the trial. Or as an alternative, with the client's consent, discuss with the opposing counsel pre-distributions from the parties' assets. So there is no misunderstanding with regard to your arrangements, prepare a letter confirming the terms of your agreement and have the client sign an acknowledgment. Don't be bashful; you are going to be devoting your heart, soul, and office to the client over the coming months, and you deserve to be paid for your hard work and commitment.

Whatever your arrangement, make sure to monitor compliance regularly. Diary internal review dates so that you can monitor compliance before it is too late for you to take action to withdraw from the case if necessary.

Review

Any great structure begins in the architect's mind, and you are the architect of this trial. What are you looking to accomplish for your client and how can you achieve it? Failing to plan is planning to fail. Work hard at the outset studying, visualizing, strategizing, and focusing on the goal to be achieved. Organize your team and identify everybody's respective roles during the process. Create your road map and start moving toward your destination.

100-Day Checklist

- ☐ Read the entire case file.
- ☐ Read the statute, case law, and secondary materials.
- ☐ Prepare a case notebook.
- ☐ Diary any critical dates and reminders 14 days, 7 days, and 1 day before the deadline.
- ☐ Prepare an outcome narrative.
- ☐ Prepare a statement summarizing the theory of the case.
- ☐ What is the theme of the case?
- ☐ What grabbers will summarize the theme?
- ☐ Prepare a narrative summarizing the desired outcome of the case.
- ☐ Perform a trial visualization exercise.
- ☐ Use the madman-architect-builder-judge exercise.
- ☐ Prepare a mind map of the case.
- ☐ Perform a critical analysis of the opponent's case.
- ☐ Prepare proposed findings of fact and judgment.
- ☐ Prepare a preliminary proof chart.
- ☐ Conduct an organizational team meeting.
- ☐ Block out weekly time between now and the trial.
- ☐ Create a notebook dedicated to preparation prompts.
- ☐ Discuss fees with the client.
- ☐ Confirm fee agreement in writing.
- ☐ Diary fee-compliance review.

CHAPTER 2
90 Days Before Trial

In many ways a trial, like skydiving, is not inherently difficult; however, both can be terribly unforgiving of even the slightest inattention.

—David Boies

Introduction

In the last chapter, I focused on using imagination and creativity—now is the time to get busy. Now is the time to make sure you have all of the necessary facts and a means to convert those facts into the evidence. In other words, what facts do you need to prove and how do you intend to prove them? Also make sure that you have complied with all rules regarding disclosures to the opposing party.

Disclosure Deadlines

When trial dates are set, request that the trial court set specific schedules for disclosures. Many court rules provide deadlines (e.g., discovery closes 60 days before trial), but it is always helpful to have the court clearly set forth dates so that everyone knows what is expected and there is no confusion or last-minute motions to continue trial. Consider asking the presiding judge to specify some of the following deadlines:

- completion of initial written discovery
- completion of supplemental written discovery
- disclosure of witnesses

- disclosure of topics of witness testimony and/or opinions
- completion of depositions
- production of initial expert reports
- production of rebuttal expert reports
- exchange of exhibits

Watching the Clock

Work backward from the date you will need information. When you serve written discovery requests, allow adequate time to compel compliance if necessary. For example, under the rules, the opponent will have a prescribed period to answer. After that, most rules require attempts to resolve differences before going to court. Next, if the matter cannot be resolved, you will need to prepare and schedule motions to compel compliance. Often, judges allow continuances of hearings. Don't let your opponents tactically run the clock—act early to request discovery in order to allow time for enforcement if necessary.

Become familiar with all disclosure deadlines in your code of civil procedure or scheduling orders of the court. If you are practicing in a location where you rarely appear, review the local court rules to ensure compliance. Use a tickler system to record all critical dates, to remind you of upcoming deadlines.

Information Audit

What do you need to prove? Do you have all of the facts to support your theory? If not, figure out what you lack and gather that information. Sometimes the information is within your client's control. Inventory what you need and direct the client to get copies of necessary information in his or her possession. If the information is not in your client's possession, figure out the most efficient way to get it. If necessary, send requests to your opponent for supplemental production of information. Consider issuing subpoenas for documents that you are missing. Don't waste time on fishing expeditions. Focus your pursuit. This is why it is critical to start with the end in mind. Pursue only the information that you need; limit your search to information to sustain the theory of the case. Your resources and time are limited—don't waste time pursuing unnecessary information.

Discovery Options

You have four options to obtain information for your case: informal methods, written discovery, third-party subpoenas, and depositions. Consider the most efficient and cost-effective manner to accumulate information for your case. Written discovery should be precise rather than generic. Seek only information you need rather than serving thoughtless boilerplate forms on your opponents.

Determine what information you can obtain informally. For example, have your client go to the bank and get copies of statements of joint accounts rather than obtaining them from subpoenas or formal discovery. On the other hand, sometimes it is simpler to issue a third-party subpoena rather than hounding a recalcitrant opponent for information. Again, what do you need and what is the most practical way to get it? Develop strategies to acquire the necessary facts for your case. Broad fishing expeditions are costly, unprofessional, and unnecessary.

Depositions

Consider what witnesses you need to depose and why. Have a plan. For strategic reasons, it sometimes makes sense not to depose a witness at all. For example, a deposition will educate your opponent concerning your theory. It also may provide a dress-rehearsal opportunity for the person who is deposed. With experts, courts usually limit their testimony to the data reflected in their report. If you depose the witness, it may allow the witness to expand the scope of his or her testimony. Weigh the dangers of deposing the witness against the benefits. Make the decision to depose a witness consciously on a witness-by-witness basis.

When you decide to depose a witness, timing is critical. Divorce litigation is not static, and circumstances evolve during the pendency of the case. Often, new information is revealed and new evidentiary opportunities unfold well into the life of the litigation. Sometimes it makes sense to wait as long as possible before deposing the opposing party, allowing inquiry into events arising during the life cycle of the case. On the other hand, as the case unfolds, witnesses become educated, and guile often follows. Timing is part of the art of trial advocacy: find the right time to depose the opposing party or other witness. And, again, sometimes it makes sense not to depose a witness at all. Trial advocacy is equal parts art and science, and trial lawyers need to use their guts to determine the "if and when" concerning the deposition.

Disclosures

In those jurisdictions requiring disclosure, be scrupulous about compliance. Disclose all potential witnesses in conformance with the rules. Err on the side of safety; you can always decide not to call the witness later. If you are not fully conversant with your local discovery rules, reread them and make sure you know all of your obligations. Here are some potential disclosure requirements:

- identity of witnesses
- subject matter and substance of witness testimony
- disclosure of expert witnesses
- expert reports
- updates to written discovery

Create a timeline and disclosure checklist. Have reminders built into the timeline to anticipate upcoming deadlines. Few things are more devastating than a self-inflicted wound concerning disclosure requirements in the rules. Courts can bar otherwise legitimate evidence that has not been properly disclosed in a timely manner. You can subject yourself to professional negligence claims as well. Make sure to comply with all disclosure requirements to avoid these unnecessary problems.

Compliance

When you receive a discovery request, diary all deadlines and determine a strategy to complete the request. Consider whether your client can independently complete the request or whether you will need to take a more active role in its completion.

Rather than sending the discovery request to the client with only the less-than-helpful instructions of "please answer these within 28 days," meet with the client and go through the request to help focus the response. Give the client a context: why it is important that the client use his or her best efforts to ensure that the answers are correct and complete, and the consequences if anything untrue is stated. Explain how the client's words can be used against him or her at trial, so your client should be as truthful and complete as possible.

Determine what you have in your possession so as not to duplicate efforts. If you already have a document, there is no need to make the client reproduce it. Make an inventory of what *specific* documents you need the client to produce and provide a date well in advance of the deadline, to allow you time to process the information. With regard to written interrogatories, you or your paralegal can answer many of them directly, limiting the client's involvement. While ultimately the client will need to sign off on the discovery, that does not mean that the client needs to formally answer every question posed. Take a more active role in discovery compliance at the outset, rather than cleaning up messes later.

As the trial lawyer on the case, personally review all responses before they are sent out. Assuming you cannot personally undertake the task, assign it to a trusted associate or paralegal. In no event should the client's answers be produced without reviewing them in detail. Avoid potential time bombs by making sure the answers are accurate, complete, and not subject to misconstruction. With regard to all documents you produce during the discovery process, keep a specific inventory of those items produced, using a Bates style stamp. Number each page produced sequentially and scan all documents produced as a single PDF (again with each page numbered) to have a complete record of the production. This will avoid claims at trial that you did not produce something.

Planning for Specific Issues

While this book cannot comprehensively address every issue that a matrimonial lawyer will confront while preparing for trial, you will regularly confront certain common issues. Consider some of the following:

General Property

Property issues in a divorce require a four-pronged analysis:

1. Identify the property.
2. Classify it either as marital or nonmarital property.
3. Once classified, it needs to be valued.
4. Determine how to equitably divide it.

Start by preparing a marital balance sheet. The balance sheet is a useful tool throughout the case, both pretrial and as a trial exhibit.

The balance sheet is a spreadsheet that summarizes the property and identifies the proposed value of the property and any issues related to classification and division. It can be amended throughout the case as discovery proceeds.

Consider establishing a separate notebook for all documents related to the parties' property. At the front of the notebook, keep the marital balance sheet with each property numbered on the sheet. Set up numbered subfolders behind the balance sheet with any appraisals or supporting documents related to the classification or valuation of each individual piece of property.

Identify your issues related to the property. Do you have any classification issues? Do you have the information necessary to classify the property? Sometimes property is acquired during the marriage with money commingled from various sources. Obtain the documents to trace the contributions to the property. Consider whether any expert testimony will be necessary to tie up ownership.

Know the date your courts use to set value of assets in your jurisdiction. For example, some jurisdictions use the date of trial as the date for valuation. If you have a value that is a year old at the time of trial, it may be subject to attack as stale. Plan ahead to ensure compliance with valuation dates. Do any appraisals need to be updated? Also, keep your eye on disclosure deadlines as you consider these issues.

Under the Federal Rules of Evidence, an owner of property can give an opinion concerning value.[1] Even so, consider whether this is a good idea from a persuasive point of view. Make sure you can properly lay the foundation for your client to testify with a lay opinion. Does your client have sufficient personal knowledge of the asset to testify credibly concerning value? If not, determine a better way of presenting valuation testimony.

If possible, set up a preliminary stipulation conference with the opposing counsel. Both you and your opponent have an incentive, on behalf of your clients, to work out agreements on noncontroversial values such as vehicles or other routine assets. Trials can be shortened by stipulations and judges certainly welcome agreements, particularly on valuation issues.

---

1. Fed. R. Evid. 701.

Income

Often, you need expert testimony to prove income for the purposes of child support or alimony. For example, determining the income of a self-employed person is often difficult because of the variety of ways a self-employed person can pay himself or herself. The issue is further complicated if the self-employed person doesn't report all income earned. If you do intend to hire an expert to prove income, start early. Meet with the expert to determine what information the expert will need to review to render an opinion concerning income. Gather any records by subpoena or through discovery. Also, when necessary, request updated information as the case progresses.

When expert testimony is unavailable or unaffordable, how will you prove income? Will you rely on tax returns alone? Consider other resources. Does the self-employed person run personal expenses through the business? If so, determine how to prove those expenses to support an argument of income beyond the W-2 or K-1 distributions.

Another approach is to prove income backward. In other words, prove income based upon expenditures. In order to do so, make sure to obtain all bank or credit card records to establish the family expenditures over a sufficient period of time. If there are other documents reflecting purchases, gather those as well. By showing what the family has spent, you can indirectly prove income. Review the data and prepare a summary spreadsheet that reflects the actual expenditures during the salient period. Optionally consider hiring a lifestyle expert to render an opinion regarding the family expenses.

Lifestyle Analysis

Related to proving income backward, you sometimes need to prove the family lifestyle. For example, you may need to establish a hefty lifestyle to support a claim of increased alimony. Or perhaps spending increased substantially as the divorce filing became imminent. Lifestyle experts are available to analyze, again based upon family expenditures, family lifestyles.[2] If you use such an expert, determine what information he or she needs to render an opinion regarding the family's expenditures over a period of time. If proving lifestyle will be

2. *See* Tracy Coenen, Lifestyle Analysis in Divorce Cases: Analyzing Spending and Finding Hidden Income and Assets (2014).

a component of your case, think about your proofs and what information you will need to gather to establish the standard of living. Do you have credit card statements, bank records, receipts, or any other documents that reflect expenditures during the period you are analyzing?

Business Valuation

Business-valuation issues are complex and usually require expert assistance. While some small businesses can be valued based upon the business balance sheet, the input of an expert is required to value most profitable businesses. To save costs, many business owners will insist on using the business accountant to provide a valuation report and testify regarding the value of the business. But there are problems using the business accountant for this purpose. The accountant is subject to impeachment based upon bias and also may not have the expertise to value a business. A CPA license alone doesn't confer a high level of expertise in business valuation. Discuss concerns with your client and put those concerns in writing. More disconcerting is the client who insists that the business does not need to be valued by an expert because of the simplicity of the operations. For the purposes of professional liability, make sure to explain, again in writing, your concerns about proceeding without expert testimony.

Assuming you need a business evaluator, don't pursue a hired gun as an expert. First, in smaller communities, judges know the "bought and paid for" experts and discount their opinions. Next, if the report is not well founded, it will be subject to attack by a legitimate counter-expert. Rather, find a knowledgeable and independent expert to assess the value of the business. Have the expert educate both you and ultimately the judge. Someone with strong academic as well as practical credentials is ideal as an expert. Often, the expert's reputation for honesty and integrity will help resolve contested valuation issues.

Sometimes, for the purposes of negotiations, an expert can provide an abridged report, giving an approximate range of values. The cost of this type of review is significantly less than a formal business evaluation because it dispenses with many of the time-consuming formalities required for a complete report to be used at trial. Consider asking your expert to provide a summary report and use it to help negotiate an agreement concerning the value of the enterprise. If a settlement cannot be reached, the expert can then proceed to prepare a more formal report.

Because of the length of time necessary to do a complete business valuation, you need to start the process as soon as possible. Early in the life of the case, determine whether you need a business valuation and discuss the process with your client. If you represent the business owner, you will have access to all information necessary for the evaluator to prepare a report. But if you represent the other spouse, getting important information may be arduous. You can't start early enough seeking the information for the evaluator.

In some jurisdictions, courts may appoint an independent expert as the court's witness. In that event, make sure there is adequate time to hire your own expert if necessary. Also budgeting issues must be discussed with the client at all stages of the case. Sometimes, as a means to save time and money, lawyers agree to hire a joint neutral evaluator to provide an opinion of value. The parties agree either to abide by the neutral's report or to allow either party, if dissatisfied, to hire another expert to refute the report.

As trial preparation proceeds, consider the benefits (or hazards) of the respective experts meeting to haggle an agreed value between them. Business valuation issues often consume substantial court time and a large part of the litigation budget. If they can agree to a value, the client will save significant fees and costs. But be careful to prepare your expert strategically to not disclose too much information, particularly if you have discovered a flaw with the opponent's report. The decision to allow this meeting needs to be done on a case-by-case basis, and the costs and benefits always need to be considered.[3]

Taxes

In divorce cases, there are usually tax issues that you must contend with. The court needs to have tax information to evaluate any property or alimony award. You need to determine how best to offer tax evidence. One option is to hire an accountant as an expert. In many cases, however, the client doesn't have the money to hire an accountant for the sole purpose of providing the court with testimony on the tax implications of a particular award. Without the benefit of an

3. Shannon Pratt & Alina V. Niculita, The Lawyer's Business Valuation Handbook: Understanding Financial Statements, Appraisal Reports, and Expert Testimony (2d ed. 2010).

expert, you need to plan, at this early stage, how you will address the tax issues. Consider the following:

- **Use of stipulations**. While you may assume that some opponents are unwilling to stipulate to taxes, don't rule it out. Remember, if taxes are an issue for you, they are probably an issue for your opponent as well, and he or she also needs to figure out how to present the evidence and arguments as well. Prior to trial or hearing, suggest a joint or cooperative approach to presenting tax evidence. Perhaps the tax analysis can be prepared by a jointly retained accountant and presented to the court as a stipulated exhibit. Or stipulations can be presented regarding the authenticity of a FinPlan report or other tax analysis.
- **Solicit judicial notice**. Lawyers often use computer software like FinPlan,[4] or similar tax-calculation programs, to calculate income taxes in various income/support scenarios. In order to present these calculations to the court, assuming the program is familiar in your community, ask the judge to take judicial notice of the tax program. If the court refuses to take judicial notice of the reliability of the program or the accuracy of the calculations, you will need to establish the reliability of the program. Contact the publisher and ask for information concerning the program that can informally be presented in support of a request for judicial notice. Otherwise, the only practical way to admit the printout is to bring in a representative from Thompson West to lay the foundation for its reliability. But as a practical matter, without a company representative, stipulation, or judicial notice, it is unlikely you will be able to authenticate the report from such a program, and you will need to consider other options.
- **Present government publications**. Federal Rule of Evidence 803(8) allows as an exception to the hearsay rule records of a public agency prepared during the ordinary course of business. Also, governmental reports are considered self-authenticated under Federal Rule of Evidence 902. The Internal Revenue Service publishes information regarding common tax issues

4. FinPlan is a program used to calculate tax implications related to child support and alimony. It is published by Thomson.

affecting divorced families. Publication 504[5] addresses the tax rules pertaining to these topics: filing status, exemptions, alimony, and property settlements. While, technically, you do not need to admit the law as evidence, these types of publications may be helpful and persuasive, particularly if a report clearly supports a position that you are advocating to the court. Even if not admitted as an exhibit, a publication may be considered by the court during the argument phase of the case.

- **Reframe the issue as legal argument**. The court must take judicial notice of the applicable law. This includes federal tax law. A tax analysis is ultimately a legal analysis. In other words, if you argue the tax implication of a particular result, aren't you really arguing tax law? Consider offering a FinPlan spreadsheet as a demonstrative illustration of your tax analysis (tax law as applied to the facts of your case), but you must get in the underlying data to make the argument. Determine all of the underlying facts a court needs to rely on in calculating taxes. For example, in calculating a potential capital-gain liability of an investment, present evidence of the tax basis (typically the purchase price) and period of ownership. If the underlying data is presented to the court as evidence, then it is only a matter of applying that data to the applicable tax law, of which the court must take judicial notice. At that point, it's only math, which can be presented as part of your argument.

Child Custody

Child custody issues require finesse due to the delicacy of the subject matter. It is always challenging to prepare a custody case while simultaneously sheltering the children from the nuclear fallout from the conflict. While some cases can be tried based solely upon the parenting strengths and weaknesses, many courts want the opinions of experts or guardians ad litem to clarify the family dynamics. These experts, often retained as the court's witnesses, will interview the family, administer psychological tests, interview collateral witnesses, and ultimately render an opinion concerning the best interest of the children.

5. *Publication 504—Main Content*, INTERNAL REVENUE SERV., www.irs.gov/publications/p504/ar02.html#en_US_2013_publink1000175898 (last visited July 27, 2015).

Review and deconstruct any child custody reports. Review the reports both offensively and defensively. Consider what information is helpful and harmful to your client and start planning how to use or neutralize the evidence. Consult learned treatises and practice books for information to make sense of the science of the report.[6] Acquire all necessary supporting information from the evaluator, including the evaluator's file and all raw testing materials. Do you need to hire your own expert to rebut any of the allegations contained in the report? Consider hiring an independent consulting expert to review the report and see if there are any procedural or substantive irregularities with the evaluation. Consultants can also be hired as litigation support, helping the lawyer formulate questions and arguments necessary to attack the adverse report.[7]

Is there a child representative or guardian ad litem involved in the case? Will you need one in the event of trial? If one has been appointed, will the guardian issue a written report prior to trial and, if so, when will it be presented? Will the representative testify as a witness concerning the best interest of the children? If the report is adverse to your client, consider impeachment options or other evidence to offset the impact of the report. Plan how you will contend with a negative report concerning your client.

Consider other potential witnesses. Have all discovery/disclosure requirements been satisfied? Has the opposing party disclosed its witnesses? Consider whether and when to depose the witnesses. As discussed, family law cases are moving targets as evidence evolves and develops throughout the life of the case. Timing is important: you don't want to depose the witnesses too early—but also not too late. Will the children be called, either for an in camera conference with the judge or as witnesses? While proper protocol should always be to minimize the children's involvement in the case, sometimes they must become involved. Determine whether and to what extent the children will be involved and prepare accordingly.

Start reviewing the journals, pictures, e-mails, and other information compiled by you and your client throughout the case. In many

---

6. *See, e.g.*, John A. Zervopoulos, Confronting Mental Health Evidence: A Practical Guide to Reliability and Experts in Family Law (2d ed. 2015).

7. David Martindale & Jonathan Gould, *Deconstructing Custody Evaluation Reports*, 25 J. Am. Acad. Matrimonial Law. 357 (2013).

cases, this compilation of information is substantial. Some clients inundate you with information during the case. Although daunting, review it as a miner looking for hidden gems. How will the information support the theme and theory of the case? Perhaps a review of this information helps crystallize things. Reviewing months of journals and correspondence between the parties is time consuming, but it is critical to look for priceless jewels in the piles of dirt. Parse through and look for the most important and salient information to incorporate into your evidence. Trials are rarely won by the quantity of information accumulated; rather, they are won by the quality and context of the evidence presented.

Evidentiary Planning

Admission of any evidence requires overcoming three obstacles: *relevancy*, *reliability*, and conformance with general evidentiary *rules* (hearsay, original writing, etc.). Relevancy speaks for itself: the proposed evidence must be material and probative of an issue in controversy. The second requirement involves the reliability of the evidence. If the evidence is not reliable, it cannot be considered. For testimony to be considered reliable, it must be based upon the personal knowledge or sensory observations of the witness. For documents or exhibits to be deemed reliable, they must prove to be real or "authentic." As part of the planning process, make sure potential testimony satisfies the personal knowledge requirement. Know the foundational requirements necessary to admit testimony regarding a conversation. In order to establish the reliability of an exhibit, be prepared to "authenticate" it. It is not a high threshold to establish the authenticity of an exhibit, but it is critical to its admission.[8]

Authentication of Exhibits

There are a number of ways to authenticate an exhibit pretrial. One method is to prepare a request to admit the genuineness of the exhibit. An admission of genuineness by a party opponent admits the authenticity of an exhibit. Admissions by a party opponent are admissible as non-hearsay. If the opponent acknowledges a document as genuine, there is no need to authenticate it at trial; the adverse

8. *See* Steven N. Peskind, The Family Law Trial Evidence Handbook 137–78 (2013).

party has admitted its authenticity already. As such, the proponent of the evidence need only address relevancy or substantive-rules objections.

As another authentication method, consider using depositions. At the deposition, ask the opponent to acknowledge the authenticity of the potential exhibit. For example, assuming you intend to offer a printout of the opponent's Facebook page for some statement made, have the opponent admit at the deposition that the printout is accurate. Often, due to the informality of depositions, the adverse party's guard is down, and he or she is more likely to admit the authenticity of such an exhibit rather than at trial, when he or she is more guarded. If an admission is made at a deposition regarding authenticity, have the deposition transcript ready at trial to show that the party admitted, under oath, that the exhibit is authentic.

If you receive a document from your opponent in response to a discovery request, it is an implicit admission the document is authentic (the opponent would have a hard time producing a document in response to a discovery request and later argue that the document is inauthentic). If you need to authenticate a document from the discovery answers, be sure to have them available as a reference at trial if the opponent challenges the authenticity of the exhibit.

Finally, solicit stipulations from your opponent concerning both authenticity and admission more generally. Also, seek judicial notice of the authenticity of the exhibit at a pretrial conference. Laying evidentiary foundations for exhibits is busy work for lawyers, but to the extent possible, do the busy work before the trial commences. Laying formal foundations at trial delays cases with tedious testimony and provides objection opportunities for obstructive opponents. If you can authenticate an exhibit before trial, you avoid giving the opponent one more opportunity for mischief.

Plan the most effective way to authenticate your evidence pretrial. Review your proof chart and determine whether any questions of authenticity exist in the first place. Often, there are none. If there is a question concerning a particular exhibit, evaluate the economics of the case, timing, and other relevant factors to determine the most efficient manner to authenticate your exhibits. Also consider strategic advantages. For example, determine whether you are more likely to get an admission about the authenticity of a Facebook printout from a surprised deponent rather than a request to admit, when the litigant and his or her attorney will have time to consult and strategize.

Also, determine the proof necessary to authenticate the exhibit. Is it a handwritten document or does it contain a signature that is in dispute? Do you need an expert witness to authenticate the handwriting? Try to ascertain any authenticity issues as soon as possible to allow you the time to hire an expert to prove authenticity.

Substantive Rules

Assuming evidence is relevant and reliable, it still must meet the other substantive rules for admission. For example, if it is hearsay, you will need to find an exception. Make sure you know the rules and prepare accordingly. Now is the time to determine admissibility of evidence, not in the heat of battle. Think hard about how you can get an out-of-court statement admitted. Weigh your options: you may need to call the out-of-court declarant rather than trying to get the statement admitted as hearsay through the witness who heard it.

With regard to business records, determine if your jurisdiction offers a certification option in lieu of calling a record keeper to lay the foundation for business records. Review Federal Rule of Evidence 902(11), which allows a record keeper to sign a certification incorporating the foundational language from Federal Rule of Evidence 803(6):

> (A) the record was made at or near the time by—or from information transmitted by—someone with knowledge;
>
> (B) the record was kept in the course of a regularly conducted activity of a business, organization, occupation, or calling, whether or not for profit;
>
> (C) making the record was a regular practice of that activity;

Under Federal Rule of Evidence 803(6) properly authenticated records of a regularly conducted activity (aka business records exception) are an exception to the hearsay rule. When Federal Rule of Evidence 902(11) is read in conjunction with Rule 803(6), a certification can be used to authenticate business records without the need to call the record keeper. Once authenticated in this manner, the records come into evidence as an exception to the hearsay rule.

If you intend to offer bank records, credit statements, or other records kept in the ordinary course of business, plan ahead and get certifications signed. If your jurisdiction doesn't have a certification option, consider other options to admit the business records, including seeking a stipulation, subpoenaing the appropriate company representative to lay the foundation, or serving a request to admit the genuineness of the documents and admitting them under the business records exception under your statute.

Review

No time to wait: there is a lot of work to do at this point. Make sure you have all of the information you will need to support the theory and the theme of your case, and then figure out how to get it into evidence. Make all of your disclosures comply with all discovery rules. If trial advocacy is both an art and a science, now is the time to concentrate on the science of advocacy: know the rules, apply them, and avoid tripping on your shoelaces because of faulty disclosures or an inability to admit a crucial piece of evidence. As the court in *United States v. Safavian* observed, failure to authenticate an exhibit is usually a self-inflicted injury.[9] Avoid self-inflicted injuries by early planning.

9. United States v. Safavian, 644 F. Supp. 2d 1 (2009).

90-Day Checklist

- ☐ Diary all deadlines with 14-, 7-, and 1-day reminders.
- ☐ If not already set by court order or court rule, request that the court set deadlines for the following (where appropriate):
  - ☐ completion of initial written discovery
  - ☐ completion of supplemental written discovery
  - ☐ disclosure of all witnesses
  - ☐ disclosure of substance of witness testimony and/or opinions
  - ☐ completion of depositions
  - ☐ production of expert reports/opinions
  - ☐ production of rebuttal or surebutter expert reports/opinions
  - ☐ exchange of exhibits
- ☐ Do you have all of the data necessary to support your theory and theme?
- ☐ If not, what is the most efficient way to obtain the information?
- ☐ Conduct a general discovery audit.
  - ☐ Have you complied with all written discovery requests?
  - ☐ Do you owe any updates to previously answered discovery?
  - ☐ Have you timely filed formal objections to improper requests?
  - ☐ Have you scheduled any objections for hearing?
  - ☐ Have you disclosed all witnesses in writing?
  - ☐ Has the opposing party disclosed witnesses?
  - ☐ Does the opposing party owe any discovery responses?
  - ☐ Do you need any updates to prior discovery responses?
  - ☐ Have you requested answers or updates?
  - ☐ Have you sent a letter to resolve differences concerning deficiencies?
- ☐ Is a motion to compel production of discovery or disclosures appropriate or necessary?

  - ☐ Do you need to depose anyone?
  - ☐ Have depositions been scheduled?
  - ☐ Is an order to compel depositions necessary?

Discovery Compliance

- ☐ Diary all deadlines with ticklers.
- ☐ Meet with client to allocate responsibility for answers/ production.
- ☐ Review client answers.
- ☐ Bates-stamp and scan completed production.
- ☐ Serve responses on opposing attorney.

Experts

- ☐ Do you need an expert for
  - ☐ valuation of real estate?
  - ☐ business valuation?
  - ☐ appraisal of personal property?
  - ☐ classification of assets?
  - ☐ tracing contributions of nonmarital property?
  - ☐ proving income?
  - ☐ proving lifestyle?
  - ☐ tax issues?
  - ☐ educating the court on a complex topic?
  - ☐ child development?
  - ☐ child custody?
- ☐ Have you investigated any potential expert?
  - ☐ If unknown, have you consulted references?
  - ☐ Have you reviewed the potential expert's CV?
  - ☐ Have you reviewed the expert's publications?
  - ☐ Have you personally interviewed the expert?
  - ☐ Have you determined the potential expert's fees?
- ☐ Have you consulted the client about hiring the expert?
- ☐ Do you have an engagement agreement with the expert?
- ☐ Are all disclosure dates known and noted in the diary?

- ☐ Have you prepared a letter to the client confirming the decision to hire (or not) an expert for the case?
- ☐ Have payment arrangements with the expert been made?
- ☐ Has the client paid the expert, or do you have an advance from the client to do so?
- ☐ Has your expert been notified of all deadlines in writing?
- ☐ Has your expert report been produced to the opposing party?
- ☐ Have you received the adverse expert's report?
- ☐ Have you received the adverse expert's CV?
- ☐ Have you investigated the adverse expert's credentials and/or publications?
- ☐ Will you challenge the expertise of the opposing expert?
- ☐ Are there any aspects of the opposing expert report that are subject to a *Daubert* challenge?
- ☐ Have you set up a meeting with your expert to review the adverse party report?
- ☐ Have you set the deposition of the adverse expert (or decided not to depose the expert)?
- ☐ Do you have to pay the adverse expert for his or her time? If so, have arrangements been made?
- ☐ Have you set up a meeting to prepare your expert for deposition?

Property

- ☐ Has a marital balance sheet been prepared?
- ☐ Have you prepared a discrete notebook or folder for the property?
- ☐ Have all assets been valued?
- ☐ How will you prove asset values?
- ☐ Have you solicited stipulations concerning asset values?
- ☐ Have all valuation experts/reports been disclosed?
- ☐ Are there any claims of dissipation or waste?
- ☐ Have you provided necessary notice to the opposing party?
- ☐ Do you have any asset classification issues?
- ☐ Have you determined your theory regarding asset classification?

- ☐ Is an accounting necessary concerning classification of assets?
- ☐ Have you researched law supporting your theory?
- ☐ Will you want to present a trial memorandum on questions of classification?
- ☐ Do you need an accounting or tracing prepared?
- ☐ Will an expert be necessary/helpful regarding classification issues?

Business Valuation

- ☐ Do you have your business evaluation report?
- ☐ Have you produced your report?
- ☐ Are any updates necessary?
- ☐ Do you have the opposing expert report?
- ☐ Have you sent the opposing report to your expert?
- ☐ Are you going to depose the opposing expert?
- ☐ If you are deposing the expert, do you have a date set yet?
- ☐ Do you have time set aside to prepare for the deposition?
- ☐ Will your expert attend the opposing expert deposition? If so, do you have good dates for his or her availability?

Proving Income

- ☐ Do you have current income information?
- ☐ What is your theory regarding income?
- ☐ Are there any undisclosed cash issues?
- ☐ Do you have
  - ☐ current paystubs?
  - ☐ W-2s?
  - ☐ 1099s?
  - ☐ K-1s?
  - ☐ individual tax returns?
  - ☐ business tax returns?
  - ☐ bank statements?
  - ☐ credit card statements?

- ☐ Do you need an expert to support your theory of income?
- ☐ Is any forensic investigation or audit necessary to prove income?
- ☐ Will a lifestyle analysis help prove income?
- ☐ Do you have all necessary records to analyze family expenditures?
- ☐ Do you intend to use a summary?
  - ☐ Who will lay the foundation for the summary?
  - ☐ Have all data relied on in the summary been tendered to the opposing party?
  - ☐ Have you complied with all rules requiring service on summary exhibits on opposing counsel?

Taxes

- ☐ Are any tax issues in controversy?
- ☐ Have you calculated the tax impact of a particular property distribution?
- ☐ Do you need an accountant as a consulting or expert witness?
- ☐ Will the judge take judicial notice of a FinPlan or similar tax-calculation program?
- ☐ Have you solicited stipulations concerning tax calculations or the foundation of a tax report?

Child Custody

- ☐ Review all child custody reports/evaluations.
- ☐ Have you requested the underlying file/testing data of any adverse experts?
- ☐ Do you need an expert to deconstruct any adverse reports?
- ☐ Do you need a consulting expert as a trial consultant?
- ☐ Do you challenge the adverse expert based upon expertise or subject matter?
- ☐ Do you have the adverse expert's CV?
- ☐ Have you obtained any publications of adverse expert's?
- ☐ Should you depose any adverse experts?
- ☐ Assuming you decide to depose the adverse expert, has the date been set?

- ☐ Has time been set aside to prepare for the expert deposition?
- ☐ Who will be your witnesses?
- ☐ Will the children testify or be interviewed by the court?
- ☐ Is a motion necessary to permit the children to testify?
- ☐ Will a guardian ad litem or child representative be necessary?
- ☐ Have you disclosed all of your witnesses?
- ☐ Do you need to update your witness disclosures?
- ☐ Has the opposing party disclosed all witnesses?
- ☐ Has the opposing party's deposition been scheduled?
- ☐ Are any other depositions necessary or advisable?
- ☐ Review all correspondence and journals provided by client.

Evidentiary Planning

Relevance

- ☐ Is the evidence material and probative of an issue in controversy?
- ☐ Is the potential evidence cumulative?

Reliability aka Authentication

- ☐ Have you served a request to admit the genuineness of potential exhibits?
- ☐ Could you use the opposing party's deposition to seek an admission regarding authenticity?
- ☐ Did you receive the potential exhibit in response to a discovery request?
- ☐ If so, can you prove you received the particular document in discovery?
- ☐ Have you solicited a stipulation regarding authenticity and/or admission?
- ☐ Will the court take judicial notice of the authenticity of the exhibit?
- ☐ Is the exhibit self-authenticated under Rule 902(11)?
- ☐ Do you have all certificates to admit business records under Rule 902(11)?

- ☐ Is witness testimony based upon personal knowledge, memory, or sensory observations of the witness?
- ☐ Have you scripted the language to lay foundation through witness testimony?

Substantive Rules

- ☐ What possible objections might the opponent raise to the offer?
- ☐ Is the evidence an out-of-court statement?
- ☐ If it is an out-of-court statement, is it exempt from the hearsay rule as an admission of a party opponent?
- ☐ Is the statement being offered for some reason other than the truth of the matter asserted (notice, knowledge, etc.)?
- ☐ Do any exceptions apply to the out-of-court statement?
    - ☐ excited utterance
    - ☐ present sense impression
    - ☐ state of mind
    - ☐ past recollection recorded
    - ☐ records of regularly conducted activity (business records)
    - ☐ commercial publication
    - ☐ statement against interest
    - ☐ residual exception

CHAPTER 3
60 Days Before Trial

Preparation is the be all and the end all of the trial lawyer. The dull it makes bright. The bright it makes brilliant. The brilliant it makes steady.

—Louis Nizer

Introduction

In the last chapter, I focused my discussion on gathering the necessary facts to support the theory and the theme of the case. In this chapter, I will discuss the organization of the information and help you develop efficient and persuasive ways to present it to the court. Final decisions need to be made on the use of exhibits and the use of fact and/or opinion witnesses. Once those decisions have been finalized, you need to prepare for your witness examination and prepare your exhibits for admission.

Address Fees

Hopefully you have addressed the issue of fees long before now, but if not, do it immediately. If you are either too busy or not good at asking for money, delegate the task or hire someone to help you deal with this aspect of the case.

If you have already made arrangements, confirm that the client is honoring the engagement agreement. If not, take action now before the train is even further down the tracks. It is easy to forget about yourself as you immerse yourself in your client's problems. Unless you consciously desire to represent this client pro bono, make sure that payment arrangements are made.

Prepare a Docket Book

While some have moved exclusively to the digital realm, most lawyers still use paper in court. Consider using a docket book during the case. A docket book is an easy way to visualize the procedural development of the case from file to trial. At the commencement of each case, place all pleadings and any court orders into a bound notebook, with an index that is updated as the case develops. Table 2 is an example of an index.

TABLE 2 DOCKETING STATEMENT

Number	Document	Date Filed	Description	Dates
A1-5	Petition for Dissolution of Marriage	12-13-14		
B 1-2	Summons and Return of Service	1-5-15		
C 1-5	Answer to Petition for Dissolution	1-20-15		
D 1	Court Order	2-4	Hearing: Set temporary support, $7,000 per month	Next date 3-15-15 for case management

The docket book is a handy reference when you go to court. You can quickly find needed information in the index. And for the purposes of trial preparation, it allows you to quickly review all pleadings and orders in a chronological sequence.

Review the Pleadings

Make sure you have properly answered all pleadings and there are no mistaken admissions in your responses. If your pleading acknowledges a fact, it is considered a judicial admission, and binding on your client. For example, if your pleading admits that your client doesn't need any alimony, the claim could be precluded at trial. Therefore, review the pleadings and make sure that all pleadings have been properly answered. In the event of an error, there is still time to seek leave to amend the pleading.[1] Avoid embarrassing or potentially fatal mistakes by reviewing the pleadings in advance of the trial.

Review all temporary orders as well. For example, sometimes issues are reserved in temporary orders to be resolved at trial. Or a temporary order may have advanced assets to a party that need to be acknowledged in the final judgment. In that event, those orders will need to be pointed out to the court at the time of trial. Generally, a review of the orders may help trigger ideas for the trial as well.

Read All Transcripts

If you don't have them already, obtain the transcripts from depositions and hearings throughout the case. If your court system does not provide a court reporter for temporary hearings, consider hiring a private court reporter to attend hearings. While every hearing need not be transcribed, the opposing party may provide helpful admissions or opportunities for impeachment that will be lost if there is no court reporter to memorialize the testimony. Likewise, if you have not done so already, order any transcripts that you will need to prepare the examination of witnesses.

Prepare Transcript Abstracts

In order to use prior testimony as an admission by a party opponent, to impeach a witness, or to refresh a witness's recollection, you will need to have a transcript from the prior hearing or deposition in advance of the trial. If possible, obtain the transcript with an index. In order to quickly access information, prepare an abstract of the transcript. The abstract is simply a summary of the important testimony, referenced by page and line number. While ordinarily abstracts are of only the adverse witness's testimony, if you have a witness who is forgetful, consider abstracting your own witness's transcript as a reference to refresh the witness's recollection at trial.

1. If you amend your pleading, the earlier "admission" converts from an unrebuttable judicial admission into an evidentiary admission that can be rebutted at trial. Steven N. Peskind, The Family Law Trial Evidence Handbook 67–68 (2013).

To prepare the abstract, read the transcript and highlight any important testimony. On a separate sheet of paper, summarize the testimony with a reference to the page and line number. For example, if the husband testifies at the deposition, "Yes, I think Sally is an excellent mother," highlight the testimony in the transcript and then on a separate sheet of paper write: *page 6/line 12 "Sally is an excellent mother.*" Go through the entire transcript highlighting and noting important testimony. Preparing an abstract also helps you find forgotten admissions or other helpful testimony to incorporate into the cross-examination of the witness.[2]

Sometimes lawyers ask an associate or paralegal to prepare the abstract as a way to help save time. I prefer to do the abstract personally whenever possible. While abstracting a transcript is often grinding busywork, it helps focus the lawyer on the testimony and provides valuable insights into the witness's testimony, demeanor, and strengths and weaknesses. When complete, place the abstract, along with the transcript, in the witness's folder in your trial notebook as a reference to use during cross-examination of the witness.

Do You Need to Rework Anything?

Review, and if necessary, update your proof chart. Review your written theory and think about your theme. Do they still make sense in the context of your preparation? If not, rework them. Your proofs may evolve and change as you approach the trial date. The critical check is always whether you have the facts (proofs) to support both the theory and the theme of the case.

Considering Your Witnesses

The choice and use of witnesses starts with an analysis of the issues involved and the proofs in the case. With every potential witness there is opportunity and danger, and you must contemplate this duality when proceeding. In a divorce case, the parties are usually the principle witnesses. But there are other possible witnesses to consider: expert witnesses, other opinion witnesses, children, and fact witnesses.

---

2. There are digital apps to help abstract depositions. Consider using iAnnotate, http://www.iannotate.com, or similar products to streamline the laborious task of abstracting transcripts.

Using Expert Witnesses

A lawyer may retain an expert to evaluate data or circumstances and to render an opinion—for example, to evaluate the best interests of a child or to value the family business. These experts rely on their observations and interpret what they see, hear, and learn through the lens of their expertise, but the expert's role is not limited to rendering an opinion on an ultimate issue. The Committee Comments on Federal Rule of Evidence 702 describe the expert's function more expansively: "an expert on the stand may give a dissertation or exposition of scientific or other principles relevant to the case, leaving the trier of fact to apply them to the facts."[3] The fields from which an expert derives his or her expertise are not limited to those areas considered scientific or technical. These experts, known as "skilled experts," derive their expertise from life and professional experience, rather than academia.[4]

For example, in a divorce case involving a family farm, a farmer who has substantial experience in farming could provide expert testimony on how farmers generate income from farming. Likewise, a financial planner could evaluate the future cost of maintaining a particular lifestyle. Following are some other examples for which a skilled expert could be retained to educate the court:

- an educator comparing competing school districts
- a police officer testifying to crime or social problems in a particular location
- a banker testifying as to someone's creditworthiness and ability to refinance property
- a college advisor testifying as to the costs and projected costs of attending a university
- a social media expert discussing the dangers of children using media unsupervised

You can also retain an expert as a consultant for litigation support. The expert is used behind the scenes to help you understand the opposing expert reports or shed light on technical or complicated material. The consulting expert helps you prepare your case for trial, without being called as a witness. In most jurisdictions, consulting

3. Fed. R. Evid. 702 advisory committee's notes, 56 F.R.D. 183, 282.

4. 1 McCormick on Evidence § 13, n.17 (Kenneth S. Broun ed., Thomson West 6th ed. 2006).

experts need not be disclosed during the discovery process. Determine as soon as possible whether an expert witness or a consulting expert is necessary or a help to your case.

Choice of Experts

Sometimes clients insist on choosing their expert witnesses. Remember, you remain responsible for the outcome of the case, and your client's choice of expert may be driven by cost or comfort due to a preexisting relationship. Discuss the strengths and weaknesses of using a particular expert. Give the client a context and explain that cases are often decided based upon the expert's qualifications. Dissuade the client from using someone less qualified or less credible. You must always remain the ultimate authority over which witnesses testify, even at the risk of upsetting your client.

Investigate potential experts yourself. If you have not used one before, ask colleagues for referrals and references. Consult other references as well. Review the potential expert's CV and determine if the expert is qualified. Personally interview the expert as well to get a sense of stage presence and whether he or she will impress the judge. Also, review the expert's publications and determine if prior publications contain opinions antithetical to the theory of your case. Determine if a potential expert witness may be a problem, before you retain him (rather than while he is on the witness stand).

Ask the potential expert about his or her retainer and fee schedule. Ask the expert the typical total cost for this type of engagement. Inasmuch as the client will need to pay for the expert, discuss the costs of the expert with the client. Obtain the client's consent prior to hiring (or not hiring) a particular expert. Make sure to confirm in writing the client's consent both to the hiring of the expert and the fact that the client understands the financial responsibility for the expert. Confirm in writing a client's refusal to permit you to hire an expert when you believe it will be necessary for the case.

Define the Expert's Mission

When using experts, define the scope of the engagement in a written engagement agreement that clearly confirms the expert's responsibilities for the case. Have the client sign the engagement agreement rather than committing yourself for the expert's fee. Of course, there are always exceptions, but as a general rule, it is the client who is responsible for the expert's fees and costs.

Make sure the client understands the financial commitment and has the resources to honor it. Nothing is more distracting than last-minute maneuverings to get your expert paid (usually a necessary linchpin to the success of the case). While not always possible, avoid last-minute distractions whenever possible to focus on the merits of the case. Explain to the client, up front, the significance of the expert testimony, the costs, and the importance of finding and committing the necessary resources.

Children as Witnesses

Parents sometimes seek to call their children to corroborate allegations. Other times, they want the child to discuss the other parent's conduct. Consider whether it is necessary or prudent to call a child as a witness. Anxiety caused to children who are forced to choose sides in their parents' divorce can be profound. Evaluate whether their involvement is necessary or whether your client is seeking validation at the expense of the child. Often, calling a child is counterproductive. Using children as witnesses offends most judges. Consider other ways to obtain the information. Seek the appointment of a guardian ad litem to interview the children and report to the judge regarding the children's observations. Or seek an in camera interview concerning the children's preferences. Consider whether you can admit statements the children made to others as an exception under the hearsay rules.[5] Always weigh the benefits against the possible repercussions of calling any witness, but particularly when calling a child of the parties.

Opposing Party as Your Witness

In some instances, evidence must come from the spouse. Decide whether you should call the spouse as an adverse witness or elicit the proofs on cross-examination. This determination may depend on whether your opponent will raise scope objections on cross-examination if you examine the witness on topics beyond those raised on direct examination. Calling the opposing party adversely is sometimes advantageous,

5. *See* PESKIND, *supra* note 1, at 75–125.

particularly if you sense that the witness, while primed for his or her direct examination, was not prepared to testify as an adverse witness. Consider calling the opposing party as an adverse witness under the following circumstances:

- When you represent the plaintiff or moving party, call the opposing party to acquire evidence necessary to sustain an element of your case. Make sure to present all of the elements of your theory during your case.
- Sometimes, it is critical to the story of the case to present the adverse party to fill in a component of the story to enhance the chronology of the presentation.
- If the opposing party is unpleasant, unlikable, or a terrible witness, presenting that witness "early and often" may help influence the judge in your favor.
- If you need to admit an admission as a component of the theory of your case.

Determine whether your rules require that prior notice be provided in the event you intend to call the adverse party as a witness in your case.

Other Witnesses

Will other fact or opinion witnesses be necessary? And if so, who are they? Determine what witnesses will help you prove your theory and support your theme. Remember, there are a number of ways to admit evidence, and witnesses are just one method. Could you better present the evidence through an exhibit or stipulation? In other words, do you even need a witness to prove a particular aspect of your case? Sometimes witnesses are necessary, not to offer substantive evidence but to lay a foundation for a piece of documentary evidence. Determine whether any witnesses are necessary for this purpose or whether other means are available to authenticate real or documentary evidence.

Evaluating the Witnesses

Initially, interview the potential witness to determine what he or she knows, what he or she can reasonably testify to, and if this witness will benefit the case. Reassure the witness that you are only looking for him or her to testify to the truth and what he or she personally knows. Confirm that you are not asking the witness to take sides—rather, simply looking for testimony regarding what the witness knows or observed. Advise the witness that you will exhaustively prepare him or her shortly before the trial and review more details about the testimony at that time.

When interviewing the witness, observe the witness's demeanor; is he or she forthright and likable? Consider whether the benefits of the testimony outweigh the risks. Is the witness friendly or unfriendly, cooperative or uncooperative? Some witnesses, such as family members, are inherently friendly, but that shouldn't end your evaluation. Clients sometimes urge you to call family members as witnesses. If the testimony is marginally relevant or cumulative, do you want to waste precious trial time? Also, consider that the hazards of mom's testimony might outweigh the benefits. Are there possible landmines? And how much weight will the judge actually give when mom gushes about her wonderful son? On the other hand, some judges are reassured by a mature presence on the witness stand. All of these considerations must be weighed when considering family-member witnesses.

Determine the availability of witnesses. Are the witnesses local and able to attend the trial, or are they in distant locations? Is the witness physically capable of coming to court to testify? Consider your client's budget and the means available to obtain alternative testimony from the witness. If the witness is not subject to your court's jurisdiction, is it possible or practical to depose the witness if trial testimony is impossible? Also consider whether it is important for the court to observe the demeanor of the witness. Are resources available to do a videotaped deposition?

Uncooperative Witnesses

Some witnesses will bluntly tell you that they don't want to get involved. Others, while not thrilled with the thought of testifying, will accept the responsibility gracefully. Some potential witnesses will take a more ominous stance and suggest in so many words that if subpoenaed, they will not be helpful to your case. Evaluate the necessity of the hostile witness's testimony. How critical is it? And if the witness really does try to sabotage the case, do you have any weapons at your disposal to neutralize the damage? Consider whether you have other safer ways to present the evidence. A person can be compelled to testify through a subpoena, but you must always consider the risk that the witness "flips" or testifies unfavorably if forced to testify. Trial lawyers often must take risks, and this is one of those occasions.

Sometimes a witness is reluctant to testify because of fear of repercussions. For example, a witness who is an employee of the adverse party may be concerned about losing his or her job if required to testify. Many of these witnesses are not opposed to sharing information but have legitimate concerns about the fallout if they do. You need to consider whether the witness, once sworn in and sitting on the witness stand, is likely to tell the truth. Choices in trial preparation always involve a balancing test. How important is the testimony? Can you obtain the information from other means? What is the likelihood the witness will tell the truth? What are the consequences if the witness lies, and do you have the ability to impeach the falsehood? To the extent that these types of witnesses will discuss their testimony with you in advance, explain the consequences if they lie under oath and their obligation to tell the truth.

Consider the danger factor with all witnesses and the possibility that a witness might inadvertently (or intentionally) sabotage your case. While there are never any guarantees, you must consider the level of risk with all witnesses. In general, when considering witnesses, consider the following:

- How cooperative is the witness? Is he or she available without subpoena?
- How accessible is the witness? Is he or she subject to subpoena?
- Will there be a cost to bring the witness to testify?
- Is the evidence available through other means (e.g., stipulation)?
- What potential risks do you have with this witness?
- What potential risks does the witness have if he or she testifies?
- Do the benefits of the testimony outweigh the risks or costs?
- Is the witness credible?

Other Considerations

Privilege

Determine if there are any privilege issues associated with the witness. Will you need to obtain any releases or waivers for the witness to testify? Do privilege claims preclude the testimony of the potential witness? You will need to evaluate the difficulty in obtaining the testimony against more efficient ways of presenting the same information.

Fifth Amendment

Consider whether any witnesses may be questioned about potential criminal conduct, which may precipitate Fifth Amendment protection. Determine the legal implications if the opposing party invokes his or her right to remain silent. If necessary, research whether the Fifth Amendment right applies to the potential testimony and available remedies in the event the witness claims its protections.[6] Fifth Amendment protections apply to nonparty witnesses as well as parties.

Unavailable Witnesses

Consider deposing witnesses who may be unavailable to testify. For example, if a witness is unwilling to travel to your jurisdiction, but willing to testify locally, determine if you can depose the witness and submit the deposition in lieu of appearing at the trial. If a witness suffers poor health, which may preclude him or her from being present at a trial, preserve the testimony by deposing the witness. Depositions are not just a means of preparing for adverse witness testimony; they can also be used to preserve the testimony of an unavailable friendly witness.[7]

Competency Issues

Are there any competency issues for the witness? Do you intend to call any young children who need to be qualified competent to testify? Do you have any impaired adults who you will call? Determine whether any potential witnesses have any cognitive or developmental issues affecting their ability to testify. Determine how to address those issues to qualify the witness. Alternatively, determine how to get in the evidence in some other manner.

Other Issues

Will you need an interpreter for a witness? If so, determine the identity and availability of the interpreter. Does the potential witness have any physical disabilities that will present obstacles to testifying? Will any

---

6. *Id.* at 213.

7. Federal Rule of Evidence 804(b)(1) that permits earlier sworn testimony by the witness is an exception to the hearsay rule. *See* PESKIND, *supra* note 1, at 111–15.

of your witnesses render a layperson opinion? If so, prepare the foundational testimony for the witness in order to do so.

Disclosure of Witnesses

If you work in a jurisdiction that requires disclosure in advance of trial, make sure you have complied with all rules regarding advance disclosure. Some jurisdictions, like Illinois, require disclosure not only of the anticipated witness but also the subject matter of the testimony and any opinions that the witness will testify to. Make sure you have fully disclosed all information that will be the subject of the testimony.

Has the opposing party disclosed all of its witnesses? Sometimes to cover all bases, your opponent's disclosure will list any and all possible witnesses, well beyond who the attorney actually intends to call. Force the opposing attorney to pare down the list and disclose actual witnesses intended. If he or she refuses to commit by agreement, file a motion and ask the court to intervene and require final disclosures by a firm date. By doing so, your investigation and depositions (if necessary) can be timely arranged and completed.

Notification of Witnesses

Notify the witnesses in writing of the sometimes overlooked details of their testimony: date, location, and other specific details of the testimony. Find out if the witness has any special scheduling issues—for example, having to pick up the children after school at 3:30 p.m. or days of the week that work better. Schedule times to rehearse the witnesses closer to the trial dates. If you do not get these appointments scheduled now, you may ignore important witness preparation in lieu of more pressing matters as the trial date approaches. And it is vitally important to the case that you spend adequate time preparing your witnesses close to the trial date.

Notify the witnesses well in advance of the trial, to allow them the opportunity to coordinate their schedule. Send a written confirmation to each witness, providing the following:

- date and time of the testimony
- exact location of the courthouse and the room number
- when and where to meet you or your assistant
- prearranged date for preparation with you or your team

- general topic of the witness's testimony
- what to do if an investigator or the opposing party/counsel contacts him or her
- necessity of your service of a subpoena

Subpoenas to Friendly Witnesses

With regard to this last point, should you issue a trial subpoena to a friendly witness? While a subpoena may be unnecessary to compel the witness's appearance, it may serve other purposes. For example, a witness may need a subpoena to leave work. Also, sometimes as an impeachment question, the opposing party may confirm the lack of subpoena and later argue that the witness appeared voluntarily "to help" you. If a subpoena is served compelling the testimony, that argument is shut down. If the witness inadvertently misses the court date, the fact that a subpoena was issued may allow a continuance or recess.

Preparing for Your Witness Examination

Once you have decided on your witnesses, set up a folder with all reference material for each witness. Ultimately, this information will be transferred into the trial notebook for use at trial. Those materials might include some of the following:

- information sheet with witness contact information
- copies of subpoenas
- impeachment materials including deposition transcripts with abstracts, interrogatories, or any other admissions
- outline of the evidence to prove with the witness
- exhibits you intend to offer through the witness

Include any documents, references, or other materials you might possibly need during the testimony.

Review your proof chart and determine the specific evidence you need to elicit from the witness. Is it complete or are there other topics or facts that you want to address with this witness? The proof chart is always evolving and needs to be constantly evaluated during the preparation process. Prepare a list of all evidence you intend to elicit from this witness. At this point, don't worry about the organization of the topics; just list the desired testimony by categories. For example, assume the witness is one of the children's schoolteachers. Here is a summary of topics to cover with the witness. The bold items refer to exhibits to be used when examining the witness.

1. appearance on school days
   a. on Monday when dropped off, unkempt
   b. on all other days, neat
2. attendance
   a. four absences, all on Monday
   b. seven times late for class, all on Monday
3. academics
   a. grades this quarter (two Cs, a B, and an A) **fall 2014 report card**
      i. confirm witness's responsibility for grading children's assignments
      ii. protocol for maintaining grades
      iii. true and accurate copy of the report card issues in the child's academic records
   b. grades last quarter (all Bs) **2013 spring report card**
4. readiness for class in the morning
   a. homework complete all days but Monday
5. child's comments
   a. complaints of being hungry on three occasions, all on Monday

This summary will ultimately evolve into your examination. Weave into the outline references to exhibits you intend to use with the witness. Also, if you have any foundational testimony necessary to admit an exhibit, reference that in the outline as well.

Structuring the Examination

Once the summary is complete, start structuring and finalizing it. Consider the order of the testimony—how to most persuasively conduct the examination for maximum impact. Consider your theme when organizing the examination. For example, if the theme of a custody case relies on a parent's selfless contributions (vis-à-vis the other parent's selfish pursuits), weave multiple examples of this conduct into the examination. Examples of conduct in a point/counterpoint format are compelling and persuasive. Use your grabber (introduced in your opening statement) whenever appropriate. Also consider presenting the testimony in a chronological "story" format. This will make the testimony more interesting, compelling, and persuasive.

Legal proceedings are stories waiting to be told. Consider the best way to tell the story with the facts of your case. Think of how great stories have moved you and, within the confines of the facts and the law, structure your examination so that you tell your client's story in a way that will move the judge to act in the client's favor.[8] Like all stories, there is a beginning, a middle, and an end to the examination.

Consider the principles of *primacy* and *recency*. Primacy and recency describe the effect the order of a presentation has on both memory and persuasion. The primacy effect refers to the fact that information presented earlier is more persuasive and more memorable than information presented later. The recency effect reflects the power of the most recent information presented. The earliest and latest information in a given presentation is the most compelling; information in the middle is least remembered.

Prepare your examination considering these principles. Start and end strong. Take for example the examination of your client in a contested custody case. Commence with compelling positive evidence about your client's strengths as a parent. In the middle of your examination, have your client admit any negatives or explain away things your opponent will highlight during cross-examination. Always confront your client's weak spots during your examination. It is always better to have the first opportunity to "spin" a problem than to reactively explain it away. Next, in the middle of the examination, explain away (if possible) your opponent's strengths, examples of evidence the other spouse will crow about during the spouse's case. End the examination by testimony highlighting the opponent's negatives and one or two final strong positives for your client. Consider a point/counterpoint recitation of examples of positive/negative conduct during this final aspect of the examination.

Keep the focus on positive evidence, emphasizing your client's strengths rather than the spouse's weaknesses. Judges want reassurance why the decision in favor of your client is the right one. The wounds from a failed marriage make many clients punitive. And while some expect vindication after a trial, that rarely occurs. The more you try to punish the opposing spouse, there is less need for the judge to

---

8. *See* Philip N. Meyer, Storytelling for Lawyers (2014).

do so. Ultimately, most judges are persuaded more by a positive presentation than confessions of the spouse's sins.

So when structuring your examination, tell a story: start strong and end strong, explain away your client's foibles, and wrap it all around the theme of the case.

Prepare Direct and Cross-Examination

Different witnesses require different methods of preparation. The level of preparation is determined by the complexity of the testimony or the importance of the witness. Always remember to keep the focus on the outcome you are seeking with the witness. What are you attempting to achieve. Work backward from that ending point.

Direct Examination

During the direct examination, the focus is on the witness telling the story. Structure the examination so the witness is onstage (rather than you). This is the opportunity for the witness to shine. Leading the witness is not only impermissible during direct examination, it is also ineffective and unpersuasive because the examiner effectively becomes the witness. Your questions should be comprehensible, short in scope, and open ended for maximum impact.

With that in mind, there are various things to consider when preparing an examination. One common approach to preparing an examination is not to prepare one—in other words, simply winging it. And while this works with a witness who is offering little substantive testimony, the drawbacks are obvious. If the witness is so inconsequential that you don't need to prepare the examination, why are you even calling the witness? At the very least, have a checklist with any facts you need the witness to testify to so nothing is overlooked.

At the opposite extreme, you can fully write out your direct examination questions. While that method of preparation provides certainty and security for the examiner (e.g., nothing will be forgotten), it has several drawbacks. First, when you are locked into written questions, you are less likely to listen to the witness's testimony and may miss opportunities for looping or improvising from a given answer. Also, eye contact is difficult to maintain when reading from a script. Maintaining eye contact helps the witness testify more naturally, and it is important that you use your eyes to help guide the witness. Also, a highly polished examination of a witness is less persuasive than a more conversational one. It is critical that you listen to the client's answers and try to develop a human connection for maximum impact.

Another approach is to work off of your outline. But again, by staying strictly with your outline, you tend to stay focused on your script rather than listen to the witness, missing opportunities to loop the testimony. Outlines also limit your flexibility, because once you veer away from the outline, finding your place becomes distracting.

Consider working from a headnote and proof format. In preparing your examination, prepare a formal outline for your examination. From there, in the sequence of your outline, list all topics that you intend to cover in a categorical manner. Within each category, itemize the evidence that you intend to elicit.

For example, assume one of the issues in the case involves the children's health. At the top of a sheet of paper, write the word "health." On the left-hand side of the sheet, write down every fact you need to elicit from the witness on that topic. For example:

1. Johnny has missed school six times this year because of illness.
2. Mollie has had four ear infections in the last 18 months.
3. Johnny has asthma.
4. Dad does not properly administer Johnny's asthma medication.
5. Dad fails to provide medicine at proper intervals.

Use the sheet as a prompt to make sure you obtain the necessary facts. You can then write notes on the sheet if necessary. This system gives you a guide to the proofs you need to adduce, but doesn't script your questions. This system allows you to focus more on the witness's testimony and less on your notes.

During your examination, start each subject by announcing the headnote, "Mrs. Jones, I want to ask you some questions about Johnny and Mollie's health," and then ask questions to elicit the necessary proofs/facts within that topic. As the evidence comes in, check it off the list. When the topic is exhausted, move into the next headnote topic and inquire regarding those proofs.

This method allows for a more natural and spontaneous interchange with the witness, keeping the judge more engaged by focusing the testimony. One drawback with this method is that it tempts you to ask leading questions. Resist! As I noted before, the focus needs to be on the witness, not the examiner. Keep the following reminder written at the top of your headnote sheet: "who, what, when, where, how, please explain." Beginning your questions with these words is a cure for asking leading questions.

Preparing for Direct Examination of an Expert

The starting point for almost all expert testimony is qualifying your expert. If an expert does not have the expertise to render an opinion, the testimony is irrelevant and the court will preclude it. Initiate your examination with a series of questions to qualify the witness as an expert. For example, solicit from the witness the following information:

- The witness has acquired degrees from educational institutions.
- The witness has had other specialized training in this field of expertise.
- The witness is licensed to practice in the field.
- The witness has practiced in the field for a substantial period of time.
- The witness has taught in the field.
- The witness has published in the field.
- The witness belongs to professional organizations in the field.
- The witness has previously testified as an expert on this subject.[9]

Your expert's credentials should dictate how much time to spend on the preliminaries. If you want to emphasize the expert's level of expertise, spend more time examining on these credentials. Sometimes your opponent may offer to stipulate to the credentials of the expert. If you want to emphasize the expert's credentials and expertise, reject the offer to stipulate and solicit testimony by the expert to highlight accomplishments.

The direct examination of an expert witness can be done in either a pyramid or an inverted pyramid format: either solicit the opinion of the expert at the beginning of the examination and recount how he or she got there or, alternatively, start with analysis and work up to how he or she achieved the ultimate opinion. This is stylistic, and you can decide what format you prefer. Either approach works. Keep in mind that the expert needs to educate the judge, concerning both

9. *See* PESKIND, *supra* note 1, at 251.

the merits of the analysis and opinion and why the opponent's is flawed or imprudent. In preparing a direct examination of an expert, it is important to include the following information in your direct examination:

- basis for the expert's expertise (academic, experience, knowledge)
- nature of the assignment (the mission)
- analysis is consistent with law (e.g., used a fair market value standard)
- what information the expert reviewed and considered
- why the expert considered that information important
- theories relied on by the expert
- assumptions the expert made as part of the analysis and why
- comparison and contrast of the two experts' assumptions and methods
- distinguish the opposing expert's analysis (why the other expert is wrong and your expert is right)
- all the steps leading to the ultimate opinion
- the ultimate opinion

Prepare your expert examination in outline format and reduce it to the headnote and proof format discussed on page 61. Great direct examinations are conversations; don't be overwhelmed by the technical nature of the testimony. Structure your examination to educate the judge on why your expert is right and the opposing expert is wrong.

Demonstrative Aids

When examining an expert, use demonstrative aids to clarify the expert's testimony. For example, consider displaying key pages from the expert's report to help explain the testimony. Or alternatively, use a whiteboard to walk the expert through an analysis that relies on a buildup method of analysis.

Preparing for Adverse Witnesses

With regard to adverse witnesses, consider whether any can be informally interviewed. To the extent that the witness will do so, arrange a time to talk to anticipate his or her testimony. Discuss the witness with your client. Perhaps your client has some insights that will help you prepare for the testimony. Investigate the witness either informally (online search) or hire an investigator to do a background check on the witness. Look for any information that may influence the testimony, such as a bias. Or look for any conduct that may subject the witness to impeachment. If possible, determine in advance the witness's general attitude and demeanor and look for any motivations behind his or her involvement. Sometimes the adverse party may call a witness that is a gift to your case.

Deposing Adverse Witnesses

Consider whether to depose any adverse witnesses. Cross-examination of a witness is much more effective if you know in advance how the witness will testify to a particular question. And the transcript can be used to impeach the witness if he or she changes testimony at trial. Also, depositions allow you the opportunity to use the adverse party to authenticate exhibits. In determining whether to depose the adverse witness, consider the following:

- the importance of the testimony for the opponent's theory
- the potential damage to your case
- the cost of the deposition and budgetary resources
- concerns about educating the adverse witness
- timing of the deposition

The question of timing is important. If the witness ends up offering helpful information for your case and damaging information for the opponent, the opponent may not call the witness, and you need to have enough time to add this witness to your witness list.

Cross-Examination

In planning your cross, first determine what you are seeking to accomplish. What are your goals? Identify the important points you expect the opposing party to make through his or her testimony and develop a plan to neutralize those points during your examination. Also, determine if you can get concessions from the witness to assist you in your case. Finally, look for opportunities to undercut the witness's credibility. In planning, consider your goals and what you want to achieve on cross-examination.

In cross, the focus is on the examiner rather than the witness. As the cross-examining attorney, you effectively testify through the questions that you are asking. Precision is the key to a successful cross-examination. Maintain witness control by asking crisp, short questions—it is the power of your questions that tells the story now. Word choice is paramount when crafting your examination. Unruly witnesses terrify many lawyers on cross-examination, but the tiger is tamed by precise questions incorporating good word choice. Well-crafted questions limit the options of an argumentative witness, and if the questions are exact, the witness's evasion is much more transparent.

Ordinarily, questions should be short, containing one fact per question. Compound questions, besides being objectionable, allow a witness to play games or evade the question. Again, word choice is critical. Avoid adjectives and adverbs that can be twisted. "Was she a *good* mother?" invites problems by virtue of the word "good." In contrast, try the following:

- She took the kids to school every day, correct?
- The children's report card reflects no tardies, correct? (As opposed to "the children have never been tardy," which again invites avoidance, e.g., "I don't know that.")
- She took the children for their regular physicals?
- You didn't take them, did you?

With regard to this last question, don't push it and ask the follow-up "and that's because you trusted her..." or something to that effect. First, that question is argumentative, and second, you probably will not get an admission but rather some double-talk about a busy schedule.

Don't try to win your case by arguing with the witness; you will probably be unsuccessful and potentially irritate the judge. Remember that the goal of cross-examination (like all other evidentiary aspects of the case) is to acquire the factual building blocks to tie up during the closing argument:

> "Judge, Mr. Jones acknowledged that my client took them to all of their physicals, while he took them to none. His conduct reflects that he trusted her judgment with regard to the children's health care. And if he argues otherwise now, ask yourself, if he was truly concerned about it, why didn't he change his schedule to attend these appointments."

Don't get greedy on cross. Get your factual admissions and then tie them up in the closing argument.

Being Precise

Inasmuch as precision is critical in cross-examination, think through your questions and write them down first in a rough draft. Analyze the questions and ask yourself how an evasive witness may play games with the meaning of the words. Actually ask the questions out loud to yourself. Contemplate how the witness might avoid the question or distort it to his or her benefit. Dump the adjectives and adverbs; any qualifying words are low-hanging fruit for the argumentative witness. Revise the questions to make sure they are bulletproof. Pare words and tighten them as you work through the draft.

Is there one fact per question as opposed to multiple facts alleged? Are all of the questions leading questions rather than open ended? Remember, control of the witness is largely dependent upon tight restrictive questions.

Anticipating the Witness

Will the witness be evasive or compliant? Will the witness be neutral or advocate. And remember cross-examination doesn't have to be "cross." With some witnesses, you can extract the necessary concessions with a smile and gentle prodding rather than with a battering ram. Consider the type of witness. Is the witness a fact witness, character witness, or an expert? Prepare your cross with this in mind.

Also remember, it is permissible to *not* cross a witness. When preparing your client, advise the client that cross-examination is sometimes best to avoid. I advise clients in advance that I may forgo crossing a particular witness for tactical reasons. There are often situations when less is more. If the witness didn't hurt your case, why expose yourself by imprudent cross? Or perhaps mom is called to testify that her son is a good dad. Is that worthy of cross-examination? And beware of being a bully if you become aggressive with certain witnesses. Sometimes it's better to simply say, "No questions, your honor."

Structure of Cross-Examination

Like a direct examination, commence with high-impact questions designed to grab the judge's attention. If during the direct examination the witness has said something that you can easily demolish, proceed to do so right away. From there, work from your theme and elicit facts to support your final argument. Start with questions that are "kills," where you are guaranteed to achieve the desired answer. By doing so, you tame the witness and set the tone for the entire cross. If you start fumbling with the witness from the beginning, you lose control and may never get it back. As Louis Nizer observed, "In cross-examination, as in fishing, nothing is more ungainly than a fisherman pulled into the water by his catch."

Also, don't cross in the same sequence as the opponent's direct examination. It will be much easier for the witness to respond if he or she is comfortable with the structure. Don't give the witness that opportunity. You choose the topics and sequence to cover—don't let your opponent do that for you. And as with direct, use headnotes to focus the examination *and* the witness. It is harder for the witness to stray when the subject matter of the examination is set forth in advance. Also, during your preparation of the cross-examination, develop a plan if the witness goes rogue or is argumentative.

Unlike direct examination, which is intended to be conversational, cross-examination needs to be precise. Writing out your questions is permissible here. Again, using the headnote category sheet, write out all of the questions and the specific response you are seeking from the witness. Make sure not to glue your eyes to your notes, however. Maintain steady eye contact with the witness as a means of controlling the witness and keeping the witness compliant.

Issues with the Adverse Expert

Typically, experts are the most dangerous witnesses you will encounter. They must be approached cautiously, but don't be intimidated. Most experts are vulnerable in at least two or three areas. Focus your efforts on those weak spots. Oftentimes, less is more with experts. And many experts' arrogance will sink their testimony. You just need to offer them the anchor to submerge themselves. This is just another witness, and if you sensibly and maintain control over yourself and the witness, you can overcome the expert. First, you need to consider whether to depose the expert.

Deposing the Opposing Expert

As with any witness, deposing the opposing expert has both risks and rewards. Weigh the benefits against the detriments when considering how to proceed. Benefits include using the deposition as a way to lock your witness into the testimony and the ability to anticipate his or her answers. By knowing in advance how the witness will testify to a particular question, you have the opportunity to tactically prepare a response with your own expert. Negatives include putting the expert on notice concerning problems in his or her report, allowing the opportunity to remedy them at trial. Another negative is that by deposing the expert, you may provide a dress rehearsal and practice fielding your questions at trial.

Don't give up too much at the deposition. Keep your cards close. Avoid pointing out the expert's deficiencies at the deposition unless you can use them to settle the case. If the expert has a glaring problem that he or she cannot remedy, consider spotlighting it at the deposition in order to settle the case.

Discuss with your opponent or the judge the possibility of allowing the opposing expert to attend the depositions. Having your expert attend the opponent's deposition will help you prepare more efficiently, rather than needing to wait until the transcript is prepared. Also, the expert can suggest follow-up questions to ask during the deposition.

Cross-Examining the Expert

Investigate the opposing expert. Make sure you have his or her current CV. Review the expert's publications and see if there may be any inconsistencies between those writings and the current report. Interview colleagues who might have had dealings with the expert and solicit any useful information to attack the report. In general, gather any information that will assist if you impeach the credibility or impartiality of the opposing expert witness. Decide early whether you intend to challenge the expertise (as opposed to the substantive report) of the adverse expert. If so, consider your options. Perhaps you could bring a pretrial *Daubert* challenge to the basis of the expertise, alleging that it is improper expert testimony. Alternatively, you could conduct a voir dire examination when the expert is tendered at the trial. Under that procedure, you have a right to examine the witness out of order on his or her credentials and can argue against qualification of the witness as an expert. Either way, plan your strategy to try to neutralize the opposing expert as soon as possible.

As trial approaches and you start preparing for the adverse expert's cross-examination, use your expert to help find weaknesses in the other expert's report. Let your expert educate you. Set up an appointment to meet with your expert to preliminarily discuss his or her testimony and the adverse expert's opinions. Discuss the possibility of potential depositions and give your expert a preparation timeline.

Preparing for the cross of an expert is arduous. These are dangerous witnesses, and your focus needs to be pinpoint sharp. Don't jump into the cage with the bear; poke him from the outside with a stick. Look for ways to confront the expert that do not require you to debate him or her on substantive points. No matter how much you study the expert's area of expertise or expert opinions, the expert will know the subject matter better than you. You don't want to get into a direct confrontation with these witnesses; you will likely lose. And when crossing an expert, do not try for a home run. Singles win ball games. Try to elicit a series of concessions that you can weave together during closing argument to invalidate the expertise or independent judgment of the expert.

When preparing, consider some of the following topics to cross-examine the witness on:

- bias (e.g., relationship with opposing party or attorney)
- concessions regarding the expertise of the opposing expert
- false credentials (e.g., memberships in societies with impressive names that admit anyone who will pay the admittance fee)
- professional reprimands or licensure issues
- contradictory statements in publications or contradictory testimony in other cases
- inconsistencies within the report
- pinning the expert down on methodologies or analysis (to be challenged by your expert)
- how the ultimate opinion would change if an assumed fact was different (use of hypotheticals)
- limitations on the expert's knowledge or experience

If you intend to use a learned treatise to impeach an adverse expert, you will need to lay the foundation that the treatise is authoritative, and you may need to use your own expert to do so.

See if you can make the opposing expert your witness. Use him or her to obtain admissions that support your case. Or, for example in a custody case, if there is some conduct of the opposing party that is not referenced in the custody expert's report and the expert has not been made aware of the conduct, have the expert opine on negative aspects of that conduct. If the opposing expert agrees that the opposing spouse's conduct is deleterious to the children, you have scored major points.

Obtain the CV from the opposing expert. Track down publications to see if you can use them to impeach the expert witness. Few things are more powerful than hanging an expert with his or her own words. If you have not already deposed the expert and plan to, now is the time to do so. While sometimes it makes sense to hold off on depositions to see if the case might settle, this strategy is dangerous—schedules fill up and people get busy and become unavailable, forcing you to scramble to obtain the date. Plus, by starting early in planning the deposition, there is sufficient time to get into court to compel a deposition of the too-busy expert witness. Make sure to schedule the expert's deposition sooner rather than later.

Preparation for Impeachment

When preparing your cross-examination questions, gather all of your impeachment materials and reference them in your notes. These materials may include prior transcripts, admissions, written discovery answers, or any other documents permitted by your rules for impeachment.[10] At the end of each written question, write down the reference to the impeachment materials you may need. For example, assume the husband admits in his deposition that the wife took the children to all of their doctor appointments. Your question might be, "Your wife took the children to all of their doctor appointments, correct?" After the question, reference the specific page and line from the deposition to use if the witness evades the question. And at trial, have all impeachment materials within easy reach. Effective impeachment is rhythmic and fluid. Impact is mitigated when there are awkward delays to find impeachment materials.

In addition to gathering and referencing impeachment materials, plan for their use. If a witness veers from earlier testimony or a written admission, how do you intend to approach the witness? I would suggest the following impeachment protocol supported by the Federal Rules of Evidence:[11]

1. Start with: "At your deposition, you testified that . . ." (differently than at the trial).

---

10. *See id.* at 278–92.
11. Fed. R. Evid. 608.

2. If the witness admits the earlier inconsistency, you are done; the impeachment is complete. If the witness does not readily admit to the earlier inconsistency, then confirm that the witness was deposed on a particular date and that the witness was sworn to tell the truth. Next, hand a copy of the transcript to the witness and ask the witness to read along with you, pointing out the lines from the transcript that you will read from out loud.
3. After you are done reading the earlier inconsistent testimony, ask the witness *only* whether you read the testimony correctly. Undoubtedly, you will get the desired "yes." This technique makes it difficult for the witness to squirm out of the earlier admission with volunteered statements with a nonresponsive "I didn't understand the question at the deposition" or "I was confused."

In order to use this system of impeachment, have three copies of the impeachment transcript with you at trial: one as your reference, one in the event the opposing counsel does not have a copy, and one for the witness to read along.

Finalizing Exhibits

Finalize your exhibits. There are two types of exhibits: evidentiary and demonstrative. Evidentiary exhibits are used as proof of any relevant fact in the case. Demonstrative exhibits have no independent evidentiary value; rather, they are used to help clarify or explain the witness's testimony. Determine the best way to tell your client's story using all available resources.

With regard to evidentiary exhibits, consider the rules regarding cumulative evidence found in Federal Rule of Evidence 403: "The court may exclude relevant evidence if its probative value is substantially outweighed by a danger of one or more of the following: unfair prejudice, confusing the issues, misleading the jury, undue delay, wasting time, or needlessly presenting cumulative evidence." If you are using a bank statement to prove the value of the account on a particular date, you don't need to also have the witness read the balance from the exhibit. Be efficient with your proofs and avoid unnecessary repetition.

After you have preliminarily gathered your evidentiary exhibits, consider the following:

- Does this exhibit help me illustrate my client's story?
- Is it relevant?
- Does this exhibit prove or help prove a material fact in controversy?
- Is the exhibit cumulative of other evidence to be presented?
- If so, is the exhibit a better way of proving the fact?
- Will a witness be necessary to authenticate the exhibit?
- Can the exhibit be authenticated pretrial?
- Are there any substantive rules that need to be overcome (e.g., hearsay, original-writing rule, privilege, etc.)?

Once you have decided on your evidentiary exhibits and planned for their admission and use, prepare a preliminary exhibit list that you will use at trial as your scorecard, allowing you to keep track of the exhibits ultimately admitted.

Consider the order that you intend to admit your exhibits when preparing your list. But don't get too compulsive about marking all exhibits chronologically. The rules ordinarily don't require you to admit exhibit 3 before exhibit 13, but it is helpful from your planning perspective to attempt to keep exhibits in the approximate order of your intended admission.

At this stage, preliminarily list all exhibits that you expect to use, recognizing that the exhibits or the sequence may change as the trial gets closer. Table 3 is an example of a simple exhibit list format.

TABLE 3

Number	Description ID	Admitted	Stip Authentic/ Stip Admitted
Pet. 1	John paystub 12-31-14		
Pet. Grp. 2	1st National Bank statements January–December 2014		
Pet. 3	Picture of Sally with bruises		

Obviously, you are free to create a format unique to your circumstances. The important thing is that you have a reference sheet that will allow you to organize and keep track of your exhibits at trial. Also prepare a template so that you can keep track of your opponent's exhibits at trial.

Planning for Use of Exhibits

Pre-mark your exhibits before you copy them. Some computer programs allow you to print the exhibit marker directly on the PDF. Otherwise, you will have to use stickers. On multipage exhibits, number all of the pages. Again consider using a Bates stamp type program to sequentially mark pages of an exhibit. During the testimony, you can then reference the exact page number you are questioning the witness about. This will save time and streamline the examination.

Make three copies in addition to the original exhibit. Use the copies as follows: the original is to be admitted and presented to the clerk, one copy is for your reference, one copy is for the opposing counsel, and one copy can be used by the judge at the bench. When you have stipulated to the exhibits prior to the trial, consider putting them in separate three-ring binders. During the testimony, reference the exhibit by number and page.

One of the advantages of early preparation is that you have the time to conduct an exhibit conference with your opponent. Many courts require them, but some courts are more laissez-faire. Request that the court order such a conference if your opponent is disinterested. A trial proceeds much more quickly and smoothly if you don't need to lay foundations for exhibits or if there are infrequent arguments concerning the admissibility of exhibits. If necessary, you can use the trial judge to rule on admissibility prior to the trial, saving precious trial time.

While you may need to argue the relevance of some exhibits in trial due to contextual necessity, most exhibits in a divorce trial are noncontroversial and can be resolved before the first witness is called. Remember that even if there is a relevance issue to work out in the testimony, you can still stipulate pretrial to the authenticity of the exhibit.

Demonstrative Exhibits

A demonstrative exhibit is used to illustrate or help explain a witness's testimony. It can also be used during opening statements or closing arguments.

A demonstrative aid is not usually admissible as proof; it simply helps the judge understand the testimony.

Think about some of the following uses when considering a demonstrative exhibit:

- Use a timeline to help the judge understand the sequence of events.
- Use a blowup from an exhibit to help illustrate a witness's testimony (e.g., a blowup of a page from the expert's report).
- Use a graph or spreadsheet to present a comparison/contrast (e.g., income then versus now).
- Use a PowerPoint during a closing argument that uses slides for law, recap of testimony, exhibit reference, etc.

While a demonstrative exhibit is not offered into evidence to prove a point in controversy, a witness will need to authenticate the exhibit. To authenticate the demonstrative aid, the proponent must establish that the item is a fair and accurate representation of relevant testimony or documentary evidence otherwise admitted in the case. The witness testifying can lay that foundation. Pre-mark the exhibit as "demonstrative exhibit number ____" and incorporate questions into your direct examination establishing that the demonstrative aid accurately represents something the witness is describing and that it will assist the court in understanding the testimony.

Often, a demonstrative aid is on a large poster board or is shown on a projector. In that event, prepare a paper copy for the judge and for the court record. If an appellate court later reviews the case, the appellate court will have a context and can review the paper copy of the exhibit referenced by the witness.

As a variation, consider using a whiteboard or flip chart when examining a witness. By selectively writing things down as you examine the witness, you visually illustrate the point you are making. Alternatively, use the prop during opening statement or closing argument to emphasize an aspect of your argument. Remember, show and tell is the mantra of all trial lawyers!

Using Summaries

A summary is a hybrid between a demonstrative exhibit and an evidentiary exhibit. Federal Rule of Evidence 1006 provides, "The proponent may use a summary, chart, or calculation to prove the content of voluminous writings, recordings, or photographs that cannot be conveniently examined in court." A foundation is necessary from the witness using the exhibit to explain how the summary was prepared and that it accurately reflects the underlying data summarized in the exhibit. Determine how you will lay this foundation. For example, if your paralegal prepared the summary, you will need to have another witness who intends to use the summary, indicate that he has reviewed the summary prepared by the paralegal, and that all of the information is accurately compiled.

Unlike a demonstrative aid, a party may offer a summary exhibit to independently prove a point in controversy. While all of the underlying documents don't have to be offered for admission, they must be admissible. A summary cannot be used as a backdoor way to admit otherwise inadmissible records. While the original documents underlying the summary need not be physically produced in court, they must be made available to the other party for inspection and copying prior to the trial. Affirmatively produce all underlying records to the opponent well in advance of the trial in order to avoid a claim of surprise. Have a paper trail evidencing the exact documents that were provided to avoid the "I didn't get that document" claim by your opponent.[12]

Review

At 60 days, the hard work of compiling and organizing the evidence is undertaken. The pieces of the puzzle should be coming together to tell a coherent and persuasive story supporting your theory and theme. Now is the time to make final decisions regarding your witnesses, exhibits, and the tone of your case. Your client's story is just about ready to be told. Prepare rough drafts of your witness testimony and compile all exhibits. Make sure all witnesses are notified concerning the dates of their testimony and the dates you intend to prepare them.

12. Fed. R. Evid. 1006.

60-Day Checklist

- ☐ Review your fee balance.
- ☐ Audit compliance with the fee agreement.
- ☐ Follow up with client if no compliance.
- ☐ Review all pleadings/orders.
- ☐ Do you need to amend or answer any pleadings?
- ☐ Prepare a docket book:
  - ☐ Compile all pleadings and orders.
  - ☐ Prepare docket book index.
- ☐ Do you have all transcripts?
- ☐ Have you abstracted all transcripts?
- ☐ Review and if necessary update the following:
  - ☐ proof chart
  - ☐ theory
  - ☐ theme
- ☐ Interview potential witnesses.
  - ☐ Consider the witnesses' demeanors.
  - ☐ Do the benefits of witnesses outweigh the risks of using them?
  - ☐ Is the witness cooperative?
  - ☐ If not cooperative, will the witness actively sabotage the case?
  - ☐ Is the witness available to testify?
- ☐ Is the witness subject to a subpoena/compulsory appearance?
- ☐ If the witness is out of state, do the costs of bringing in the witness warrant the price?
- ☐ Do the benefits of a deposition of an out-of-state witness warrant the costs of traveling to depose the witness?
- ☐ Is a video/closed-feed deposition an option?
- ☐ Can you use a deposition to authenticate potential exhibits?
- ☐ Should you depose any of your own witnesses if potentially unavailable at trial?

- ☐ Do you have any privilege issues to contend with?
- ☐ Do you need to obtain any releases or waivers for the testimony?
- ☐ Do you anticipate any Fifth Amendment issues for your witnesses?
- ☐ Do you expect any Fifth Amendment issues for opposing witnesses?
- ☐ Will you call any child witnesses?
- ☐ Will you have any competency issues?
- ☐ Will you be seeking an in camera interview with the children?
- ☐ Will the opposing party seek an in camera interview?
- ☐ Are any preliminary motions necessary regarding a child witness?
- ☐ Have you disclosed all of your witnesses?
- ☐ Have you received disclosures from the opposing party?
- ☐ Will you depose any adverse witnesses?
- ☐ Have you scheduled those depositions?
- ☐ Are all of your depositions complete?
- ☐ Have you analyzed whether to depose the opposing expert?
- ☐ If you are deposing the opposing expert, have you scheduled the deposition?
- ☐ Schedule time to prepare for the expert deposition.
- ☐ Can you informally interview any witnesses disclosed by the opposing party?
- ☐ Do you need to formally investigate any opposing-party witnesses?
- ☐ Have you discussed the adverse witnesses with your client?
- ☐ Have you sent written confirmation to your witnesses regarding the following?
    - ☐ date and time of the testimony
    - ☐ location
    - ☐ where and when to meet
    - ☐ prearranged date for preparation and rehearsal

- ☐ general topic of testimony
- ☐ instructions if contacted by opposing party, attorney, or investigator
- ☐ explanation regarding subpoena

☐ Prepare subpoenas to the following:

- ☐ ______________________________
- ☐ ______________________________
- ☐ ______________________________

☐ Are the subpoenas served?

- ☐ Subpoena served on ____________________ this date ____________.
- ☐ Subpoena served on ____________________ this date ____________.
- ☐ Subpoena served on ____________________ this date ____________.

Witness Preparation

☐ Compile all documents related to witness testimony, including the following:

- ☐ information sheet
- ☐ copies of subpoenas
- ☐ impeachment materials
- ☐ witness outline
- ☐ examination of each witness

☐ Prepare outline/structure of direct examination of all witnesses.

☐ Reduce outline to headnotes and proofs.

☐ Prepare cross-examination questions in rough draft.

☐ Rework cross-questions.

Exhibits

☐ Compile evidentiary exhibits.

☐ Pre-mark exhibits.

☐ Copy and bind exhibits.

- ☐ Prepare exhibit list.
- ☐ Prepare blank exhibit list for opposing-party exhibits.
- ☐ Authenticity established?
- ☐ Schedule exhibit conference with opposing counsel.
- ☐ Do you need to ask the court for exhibit conference?
- ☐ Would a demonstrative exhibit clarify witness testimony?
  - ☐ timelines
  - ☐ charts or graphs
  - ☐ blowups
  - ☐ poster boards
  - ☐ PowerPoint
  - ☐ whiteboard or flip chart
- ☐ Are you using any summaries?
- ☐ Have you provided all documents summarized?
  - ☐ Who will lay the foundation for the summary?

CHAPTER 4
30 Days Before Trial

I'm a big believer in the fact that life is about preparation, preparation, preparation.

—Johnnie Cochran

Introduction

If the suggested timelines in the book have been followed, most of the heavy lifting should now be done: your proofs have been culled; your exhibits have been pulled, collated, and prepared; your witness examination outlines are complete; and you are now calmly awaiting the battle. If not calmly waiting, hopefully you are at least not panicking and scrambling to get ready. All of the hard work up until now should improve the final moments leading up to the final court dates.

Assuming all other tasks are done: finalize your trial notebook, prepare your opening and closing arguments, consider whether any pretrial motions may be necessary, prepare for final pretrial conferences, and formally prepare your witnesses for their testimony.

Manage Your Calendar

Look at your calendar. Are days blocked for both the trial itself as well as time to interview witnesses or otherwise prepare? Do a memo advising your team of your anticipated schedule for the upcoming month and ask everyone to keep you clear with any major commitments. The last thing you need is a major deposition or an important contested hearing the day before your trial is to commence (although you will be ready at that point!). If things need to be rearranged, you will now have plenty of time to rearrange things. Also, discuss the upcoming dates with your spouse and family to ensure there are no avoidable personal commitments that might interfere with the court dates.

Prepare a Trial Memorandum

While some judges or local court rules require presentation of a trial memorandum, other courts are more informal. Consider using one, particularly when a judge is not likely to allow you to make an opening statement. The benefit to preparing such a memo, in addition to the opportunity to advocate, is that it helps you think through the case prior to finalizing your preparation. Obviously, if the court provides a structured format, follow that. If not, consider including some of the following information in your trial memorandum:

- any legal research pertinent to the issues in the case
- a summary of the issues in dispute
- a summary of noncontroversial/undisputed facts
- a summary of witnesses disclosed by both parties
- proposed exhibit list
- any stipulations already reached or sought

Trial memoranda can help judges focus on what you deem to be the important aspects of the case, and they should be used when permitted. When your rules don't specifically provide for a memorandum, obtain prior leave from the judge to present such a memo to avoid claims by less prepared lawyers that an unsolicited memo is improper. Most judges will appreciate the summary and review it.

Finalize the Notebook

There is no absolute for the physical structure of a trial notebook. I use a three-ring binder (or binders) at trial. Others prefer color-coded folders. Still others may prefer a digital format, using their laptop or other digital device as a virtual notebook. Regardless of the format, it must be uncomplicated and effortless to use.

Trials involve many moving parts: observing the witnesses, fielding objections, managing the client, and frequently, other unexpected surprises. The trial notebook is an antidote to some of the chaos. By knowing precisely where a specific item is, you reduce a substantial obstacle to success. Use your brain to evaluate the testimony rather than worrying where a particular piece of paper lies.

Start finalizing the trial notebook with the thought of using it at trial. Compile all information you may rely on, not just evidentiary information. For example, in jurisdictions where courts limit evidence to items previously disclosed in the discovery process, a reference of those items produced should be placed into the notebook to thwart last-minute claims of surprise. Every case is different, the issues and obstacles vary, and the notebook needs to accommodate the unique aspects of every case. Here are some things to consider in developing a final trial notebook:

- **Outcome narrative**. At the front of your notebook, put your outcome narrative, which you prepared when you started preparing for trial. This puts your goal up front, as a regular reminder of what you are trying to achieve.
- **Miscellaneous**. Reminders for yourself go here—for example, witnesses that need to be called out of order, scheduling, court reporter phone numbers, etc.
- **Factual summary**. Prepare a one-page summary of important facts for a quick reference at trial. For example, include important dates, names and ages of children, and any other information that you might reasonably need to access throughout the trial.
- **Theory and proofs**. Have a section in your notebook for a summary of the theory of your case and the critical facts you must prove to sustain the theme or theory of the case. Make sure you refer to this document throughout the trial to make sure everything that you need is coming in as necessary. And certainly don't rest your case until you have reviewed the document to make sure everything necessary has been presented.
- **Key pleadings and orders**. Have a section with copies of the important underlying pleadings. In many matrimonial cases, many pleadings are filed during the pretrial phase of the case. Use your judgment regarding which pleadings and orders to bring in the trial notebook. At the very least, have physical or digital copies available in the event you need to refer to an earlier pleading. In a complicated case with many pleadings, consider using a separate docket book instead (see page 46).

- **Motions in limine**. Place any motions in limine and orders disposing of same.
- **Trial memorandum**. If you have prepared a trial memorandum, include a copy of the memo as a reference.
- **Discovery references**. Include summaries of all information provided during the discovery cycle of the case and any pertinent discovery documents you might need to reference during the trial.
- **Opening statement**. Depending on whether you work from an outline or a written script, have the document in a section in the trial notebook.
- **Individual witnesses**. Have a separate section (or notebook) for individual witnesses that you intend to call and those witnesses you anticipate the opponent will call. Hopefully, your rules provide advance disclosure requirements to avoid surprises. Generally, there are five types of witnesses: your client, the opposing party, general fact witnesses, lay opinion witnesses, and expert witnesses. The folder for each witness will vary with the type of witness. In the section devoted to your client, have the outline of the proofs that you will elicit through your client's testimony. Have a list of any exhibits you intend to admit through the witness's testimony. Also have the client's discovery answers or deposition transcript to review in case your opponent tries to impeach your client during cross-examination. Include your general outline of the direct examination and any other notes or references that might be needed during the testimony.

With regard to the section devoted to the opposing spouse, have your outline of the cross-examination. Also, have any impeachment references available: admissions, transcripts, interrogatory answers, etc. Nothing impedes an adverse examination more than having to stop and find the appropriate impeachment reference. Success at trial is dependent upon good rhythm and timing, and those references must literally be at your fingertips.

For other witnesses you will call, include your outline and notes of the direct examination of the witness. If it is the opposing party's witness, include any impeachment information necessary to cross-examine the witness. Include your outline of the cross-examination points of the witness. Finally, if you intend to offer exhibits based upon the testimony of the witness, prepare a summary checklist to make sure you cover the necessary foundation for the admission and admit the exhibit.

- **Law**. Bring any statutes or case law that you might need at the trial. If you anticipate arguing a particular point, bring copies of any reference materials for the judge and your opponent. If you anticipate an evidentiary challenge, have any evidentiary resources (case law, etc.) available in this section. Make multiple copies of legal reference material. Staple to the front of your copy of the case a summary of the holding or language and the page number of any cites you may need. Highlight the important text in the copies of the cases as well. Affix clips or sticky notes to quickly get to the language from the decision.
- **Closing argument**. Judges differ on closing arguments. Some will request written closings within a few weeks after the completion of the evidentiary phase of the case, others will want an oral closing, and still others may want a combination of the two. If you anticipate giving an oral closing, use this section to summarize your arguments or outline the actual closing. Obviously, if you rely on case law or other reference materials, include those either in this section or in the law section discussed in the previous paragraph.
- **Exhibits**. Have a section for your and the opposing party's respective exhibit lists. (See page 72 regarding exhibit lists.) Rather than keeping copies of all of your exhibits in the trial notebook, keep a separate folder for all of the exhibits.

The key is to make the trial notebook functional and easy to use. Use an index to quickly find sections. Use sticky notes or any other device that will help you quickly get to key information. Make sure the form of the notebook is easily accessible in the heat of battle. Again, utility is critical: don't stuff too many documents into a three-ring binder, limiting your ability to turn the pages. Perhaps you want to have witness reference materials in a separate binder. Again, the notebook is about function, not beauty. Determine the structure that works best for you.

Prepare Your Opening Statement

Many judges conducting bench trials don't want to hear an opening statement. After nursing a case for months and sometimes years, a judge may find the opening an unnecessary time waster. But as an advocate, urge your judge to allow a brief opening statement to set the stage for the case. Remind the judge that while he or she may know many of the facts and have some familiarity with your theory, the opening summary will help him or her understand the case in context. But don't press. Gauge the level of your judge's reluctance prior to the trial. If the judge remains steadfast, use your trial memorandum as your opening; it can serve the same purpose—to introduce the judge to the theory and the theme of the case. Just make sure to get it to the judge before the trial so he or she has time to review it in advance.

If you are permitted to present an opening, do so. Many lawyers (often because of a time crunch and lack of time to prepare) waive the opening statement. Frankly, other than situations in which the judge will be peeved, there is no reason to waive an opening statement: it is an opportunity to set the stage, introduce the theme and theory of the case, and present a context for the evidence to come. As trial lawyer and professor Michael Tigar observes, "deciders perceive whole stories." And the opening is the opportunity to encapsulate the whole story in a few words.[1] An effective opening has an added benefit: it serves as a shot of adrenaline for the advocate, quelling the nausea that often accompanies the commencement of a trial.

Opening statements don't need to be long to be effective. As in so many instances of trial advocacy, less is oftentimes more. Keep it simple; you are introducing the judge to your case, not exhaustively reciting every fact to be presented in the coming hour or days. Start strong with a grabber: "Judge, this case is about a father's love—a father's love for money and control." From there, lay out the theme and theory in the context of the evidence to be presented. "We will present evidence showing that the motives behind Mr. Jones's claim for custody are financial, not the best interests of these children." Then proceed to cover the principal factual highlights of the case in this context.

Remember, an opening statement is not argument, and when preparing, focus on introducing the evidence rather than interpreting or

1. Michael E. Tigar, Examining Witnesses 5 (2d ed. 2003).

arguing it. That is not to say that the opening is a benign recitation of facts. Order the facts so that they are compelling and persuasive support for your theory of the case. Cognitive psychology tells us that the best way to process information is through storytelling; tell your story through the facts you intend to present. Make it chronological and understandable. Use vivid and interesting language and don't be redundant or repetitive.

Consider the use of demonstrative exhibits. For example, if your case involves a complicated tracing of assets, you may be better able to present the evidence to come with a visual aid or timeline. If you do intend to use a demonstrative exhibit, consider the type of aid: a preprinted poster board, a flip chart that you can write on, or a projector with a screen. Plan ahead for the medium you will use and make sure your team or you have the exhibit and the medium coordinated prior to trial.

It is proper to discuss the facts without qualifying the evidence. In other words, you don't need to recite the words "the evidence will show" with each fact presented. This type of redundant qualifier makes the presentation choppy and unnatural. Ideally, prepare your opening so that you can present it without notes; by doing so, you will enhance your effectiveness. Take the time to do this.

Talk to the judge as a human being; don't be an automaton reading a script. Connecting your theme with the judge early in the case is critical to a successful result. Also, don't underestimate the power of eye contact in all aspects of trial advocacy. Look at the judge while presenting your opening. When preparing, memorize the key points: this will allow a more natural presentation than reading from a script. Practice your delivery: concentrate on speaking slowly and clearly. First impressions are critical, and this is your first opportunity to shine on behalf of your client!

Prepare Your Closing Argument

You come full circle with the closing argument. The closing allows you to tie everything up and make sense of the evidence in the context of the theory of your case. All of the examinations and procedural maneuverings lead to this moment. In chapter 1, I recommended starting your preparation with the closing; if you did, pull out your notes and finalize the outline based upon all of your preparation since then.

If the judge offers you an option between writing your closing or giving it orally, consider the nature of the case and the issues. More complex financial cases lend themselves to a written closing. Custody cases, or other cases that involve an emotional or fairness component, are better served with an oral closing. Also, you may be a better writer than your opponent. Consider the cost (written closings usually take more time to prepare). Determine the most effective medium considering the issues and circumstances of your case.

Regardless of the form, start preparation by brainstorming all of the elements that you intend to address and consider the best manner to approach the argument. Also, this is the time to focus on the heart of your case, how best to communicate the emotional gravity of your position. Consider how you can weave your theme with the evidence and the law. Evaluate the most compelling structure in which to present it to the judge. A closing argument must combine the evidence, law, and appeals to fairness, and all of those elements need to be raised in your closing argument. Contemplate why your requested relief is the right thing for the judge to embrace, and figure out the best way to communicate that.

While it is tempting to focus on the sins of your opponent, structure your start with the strengths of your client and the positive merits of your case. A closing argument that parades your opponent's indiscretions is less effective than one that focuses on your client's strengths. It is those strengths that will move the court. That is not to say that the opponent's weaknesses should not be addressed—they must be exposed for the greatest impact—but don't make them the primary focus of the argument.

Consider preparing a visual aid to accompany the argument. Use the exhibits to help clarify or punctuate the argument. Or create demonstrative aids to help tell the story. The great Chicago trial lawyer Dan Webb says, "visual aids can make or break a trial."[2] These props don't need to be extravagant or intricate; they are simply tools to help the judge better process and remember the evidence and the arguments. Visual aids add color to your presentation. Like the rest of us, judges live in a visual society, and a presentation that incorporates

---

2. Charles P. Kocoras, May It Please the Court: A Story About One of America's Greatest Trial Lawyers (2015).

visual elements will make it more interesting and thus more persuasive. Consider using a whiteboard or flip chart to write on during your closing. As another technique, consider using PowerPoint slides to accompany your closing argument. Be creative: think of the elements of the case that you can visually present. For example, you can project key documents you want to highlight, the first page of seminal cases, pictures admitted during the case, copies of the transcript with important testimony highlighted, or other impactful aspects of the case.

Practice your presentation. Use your family or staff to critique your closing. Focus on the pace and rhythm of the argument. Ask for feedback from your audience. The closing is your last chance to advocate your client's case, and you need to hit a home run with it!

Prepare Final Pretrial Motions (Motions In Limine)

Consider whether a motion in limine is appropriate or tactically a good decision. In planning, always remember you are trying your case to two courts: both the trial and appellate court. If issues are not first raised in the trial court, they may be barred in the appellate court. A motion in limine is an effective way to raise the issue so that, if unsuccessful, it can be preserved for review in the appellate court. It also allows you to raise issues pretrial to avoid burning precious trial time arguing about them.

You can file a pretrial motion seeking a ruling concerning the admissibility or inadmissibility of a witness or a particular piece of evidence. Here are some topics to consider regarding such a motion:

- If multiple witnesses disclosed in discovery will be cumulative on a given point, use a motion in limine to bar cumulative testimony.
- Use a motion to bar presentation of evidence or issues not properly disclosed pretrial.
- Sometimes, lawyers prepare a witness disclosure listing many potential witnesses. Use a motion in limine to force the opponent to pare down the witness list.
- If certain information was not disclosed in discovery on a timely basis, use a motion to bar the evidence at trial.

- Use a motion to have the admissibility of prospective evidence ruled on in advance to save the cost of bringing in witnesses.[3]
- Consider using a pretrial motion to determine anticipated claims of privilege.
- Use a motion in limine requesting that the court take judicial notice of certain evidence.
- If you have scheduling issues with witnesses, use a motion to seek leave to call a witness out of order.
- Use a motion in limine to bar witnesses from observing other witness testimony or allow an expert witness to observe the opposing expert's testimony.

Often, lawyers will wait until immediately before the trial to present the motion, but there is no need to wait. Prepare and, if possible, schedule the motion for hearing as soon as possible to allow you the opportunity to plan based upon the ruling.

Prepare for Final Trial Conferences

Many courts conduct final trial conferences shortly before the trial. These conferences serve a number of purposes: to solicit stipulations, to gauge the length of the trial, and to discuss settlement and any other topic that your trial judge wants to discuss. Use this conference efficiently. If there are topics you want to address with the court, such as a request for judicial notice or other procedural relief, bring any authorities and provide them to your opponent prior to the conference.

Use the final conference to deal with evidentiary issues. If you have pretrial motions concerning the evidence, seek to have those heard at the conference to avoid unnecessary court appearances during the final countdown. Ideally, all exhibits should be exchanged and reviewed prior to the conference, and the court can determine whether any evidentiary controversies exist. Even if your opponent does not provide his or her exhibits in advance, provide your exhibits so that you can determine, with the judge's help, if your opponent will raise any objections to any of them. The court can rule on those disputes at the conference and save valuable trial time. Make sure

3. In some instances, courts may deem such a ruling advisory in nature. Consult your local case law and rules.

to draw an order incorporating any agreements or rulings from the conference. By doing so, you will preserve your record in the event of an appeal, and also, you will avoid confusion or misunderstanding at the trial.

Ask the judge his or her preferences regarding the admission of exhibits. Does he or she want copies separate from the originals? It is good practice to offer the judge copies that he or she can keep at the bench or take into chambers for review. Also, ask the judge if he or she wants you to highlight the critical text in exhibits for quick review. Discuss the judge's particular preferences so that you can conform with them.

If your client needs accommodations, advise the judge at this time. Notify the judge if you expect to use an interpreter. If certain health issues affect your client, point those out. For example, your client may have back problems and need to stand to stretch.

Many lawyers who have thwarted your efforts to discuss settlement for months will appear at the final conference unprepared and attempt to settle the case. This last-minute interest in a dialogue can be maddening, but maintain self-control and evaluate the offer. Since you will be prepared, you don't need to cave in at the 11th hour. If you are ready and your opponent is not, don't let the opposing lawyer use the conference to squeeze unreasonable concessions from you.

Finalize Witness Preparation

In his book *Preparing Witnesses*, Daniel Small summarizes the seven mistakes lawyers make when preparing witnesses. Categorically, they are the following:

1. I'm too busy.
2. The client is too busy.
3. All witnesses are created equal.
4. You never know what they'll ask.
5. Preaching, rather than teaching.
6. The law is the law.
7. Do I need to draw you a road map?[4]

---

4. Daniel I. Small, Preparing Witnesses 42–47 (4th ed. 2014).

I'm Too Busy

Daniel Small stresses the importance of witness preparation, a subject most lawyers take for granted. Who isn't guilty of telling clients to meet a half hour early before a deposition or important hearing so that you can prepare? According to Small, a lackadaisical approach to witness preparation is malpractice. Adequate time must be reserved well in advance of the hearing to prepare the client. And if the incremental preparation suggestions in this book are followed, there should be plenty of time to prepare your witnesses.

The Client Is Too Busy

Sometimes, you have to deal with your clients' reluctance to spend the necessary time due to their busy schedules. Sometimes, clients just don't want to be inconvenienced. Regardless of the client's reasons, pursue and persist. Emphasize how critical the preparation process will be to a successful result. Put your foot down and insist that the client set aside the time to meet. Work with the client to accommodate his or her schedule. If necessary, stay late or meet on the weekend. One of the great byproducts of early trial preparation is that you have extra time rather than needing to use every spare moment to prepare last minute. Most of your workup is done. Now force the client to take the time and make it happen.

All Witnesses Are Created Equal

Another mistake includes the assumption by the lawyer that all witnesses are alike, and therefore a generic approach to witness preparation is sufficient. It should go without saying that each witness is different and deserves to be treated individually. You would not prepare the busy homemaker the same way you would the sophisticated CEO. You need to thoughtfully approach your task on a witness-by-witness basis.

You Never Know What They'll Ask

Don't be guilty of "learned helplessness" or a refusal to prepare the client because you don't know what the opposing counsel will ask. Small suggests challenging yourself by walking in your opponent's shoes. What questions would you ask if you were in his or her place? While you may not know all of the questions, a quiet reflection on the opponent's theory, argued in pretrial conferences and the courthouse hallway, will provide insights into the topics that will likely be covered.

Preaching, Rather Than Teaching

Another mistake is to force-feed the witness. In other words, don't cram the preparation down the witness's throat. Rather, take your time to understand and listen to the witness. Ask questions and listen to the answers. Answer the witness's questions and try to determine his or her concerns. Figure out the best way to convey the techniques and strategies to enhance the witness's presentation on the witness stand.

The Law Is the Law

Small also advises against forgetting that the legal system is terrifying for most people. When working with witnesses, remember that court is considered a dangerous and unforgiving land, which requires a confident tour guide. Take your time to explain things in plain English, rather than in incomprehensible legalese. We sometimes forget that ordinary people don't speak our language. Translate the process into terms the witness can easily understand. Make sure the witness knows in advance the process, procedures, and protocol before he or she takes the stand.

Do I Need to Draw You a Road Map?

A detailed road map is exactly what the witness needs to succeed. Provide a detailed step-by-step tutorial. Small suggests starting with the basics: "who, what, when, where, and how" when preparing the witness. Start to finish, draw a detailed diagram of the terrain for the witness.

Prepare Your Client for the Trial

Presenting your client in a favorable way is vital to a successful result, and it is the rare divorce trial that the client is not at the top of the witness list. Preliminarily, give your client an overview of the procedures and protocol of court. The odds are good that the client has never formally testified at length before. Spend the time to educate your client and help him or her feel more relaxed. Walk the client through the trial, from opening statement to closing. Explain the mechanics of trial procedure in general terms. Advise the client of your role at trial and what you will be doing. Discuss how objections work and how to handle questions from the opposing counsel. Advise the client that you will meet with him or her closer to the trial to rehearse testimony and answer more-detailed questions regarding testimony.

Explain that the opposing attorney may call him or her as a witness. To give your client a context, explain the rules, reasons, and procedures related to calling an adverse party as a witness. Try to anticipate the topics that might be raised during the adverse examination and plan strategies on how to best counter them. By advising the client of the possibility in advance, it will help avoid potential calamities brought on by surprise and the resulting nerves.

Discuss your client's wardrobe at trial. Tell the client to dress respectfully. This means that the client shouldn't dress too casually or uncomfortably formal either. Consider your issues. If you represent dad in a contested custody case, have him dress more like a stay-at-home parent than a suave bachelor. If you are defending a business owner who is claiming hard times, tell her to leave the TAG Heuer off her wrist. Think about how you want your client to appear and discuss wardrobe options.

As noted, start with the basics and speak in terms your client will understand. Draw a diagram of the courtroom for the client. Show where he or she will sit in relation to the judge, clerk, and the lawyers. If possible, arrange for a field trip—either you or a team member should meet the client at court a few days before the trial to show your client exactly where everything is located. Identify where the lawyers will stand when asking examining witnesses. Explain where the client will sit when he or she is not testifying, and that he or she will still be onstage, even when not on the witness stand. Point out that the judge will observe his or her demeanor, facial expressions, and conduct throughout the trial and that the client should maintain a calm and composed demeanor at all times. Urge the client to remain imperturbable even if he or she hears lies or other upsetting testimony during the case.

Explain your role at the trial and how critical it is for you to concentrate; therefore, urge the client to write down comments or questions rather than speak to you while the trial is in progress. Give the client a context: describe what you will be doing at the trial. I explain that when I am not examining a witness, I am listening to the other lawyer's examination both with my ears and my eyes, watching both the witness and the judge's body language as he or she reacts to the testimony. I explain that I am simultaneously listening for objectionable testimony or planning my response to the testimony. I am also evaluating the evidence to see how I can use it as part of my closing argument. In order to do this, it is vital that the client not disrupt my concentration. Advise the client to bring pen and paper for notes, but make sure to bring some extra with you in case the client forgets. Assure the client that you will review his or her notes at convenient times and that the client must write legibly so you can understand his or her comments or questions.

Walk the client through the proceeding. Break it down. Explain where and when he or she should meet you before the trial. Don't overlook basics: make sure the client knows the courtroom number and the time the trial is to commence and what time it will recess. Estimate how many days you expect the trial to last. Describe the sequence of the trial: the case starts with brief opening statements by the attorneys, then the client and the other witnesses will testify, the lawyers will give their closing arguments, and then the judge will rule. Explain all of the parts of the trial and the significance of each part. Make sure to solicit questions from the client as well.

Identify others who will be present at the trial: the clerk, the bailiff, and the court reporter and their respective roles. If you know your judge, give the client some information about the judge: background and general temperament. Explain the judge's role beyond being the ultimate decider. Tell the client that the judge's job is to make sure the trial is fair and he or she will maintain order and appropriate decorum. Also explain that the judge's rulings on objections is not an indicator of the ultimate result and not to panic if evidentiary rulings tend to favor the opposing party. By giving the client as much information as possible, you will help empower him or her and help ease some of the pretrial jitters.

Advise the client of the break protocol (e.g., that the judge will usually break roughly two hours into the case) and what to do if the client needs an emergency bathroom break. Determine if the client has any blood sugar or other health problems and whether more regular breaks will be necessary. Does the client need any special accommodations in the courtroom? If you will need an interpreter or other translator, make sure to arrange for one well in advance. Finally, determine whether water will be available. If not, advise the client to bring a bottle or provide one as a courtesy.

Prepare the Client to Testify

Start by explaining that both you and the opposing attorney will ask your client questions during the trial. Advise him or her that sometimes the judge may ask questions as well. Regardless of who asks the client a question, he or she should follow the same practice:

- Listen to the question asked.
- Take a breath and think about the question.
- If he or she does not understand the question, say so.
- If he or she does understand the question, answer it.

Tell the client to take his or her time with the answer; there is no rush. Remind your client not to think out loud before answering the question—formulate the response in his or her mind before speaking. Point out that we have all said things in our life without thinking first, and the courtroom is not the place to do that. Think first and then answer, not vice versa.

Emphasize that the client should only answer the question asked—to listen closely and think about it before answering. If the question calls for a yes or no response, answer "yes" or "no," nothing more. For example, if asked whether Sally ever babysat for the children, the response should be yes or no, not that "she is 23 years old, certified in CPR, and is in medical school." Advise the client that judges get irritated when the witness rambles beyond the actual question, so he or she should be as precise as possible. Explain that sometimes lawyers will ask confusing questions and that if the client doesn't understand the question, he or she should speak up rather than trying to guess what the lawyer is getting at. Make sure the client doesn't inadvertently step on a land mine because he or she feels stupid asking for clarification; explain that most lawyers are not trying to trick the witness but inadvertently ask jumbled questions. The motto should be: when in doubt, say so!

Advise the client that it is improper to testify with a guess, but an educated estimate is appropriate under some circumstances. In the event the client is giving such an estimate, he or she should say so: "I'm not 100 percent certain, but I think we had between $50,000 and $60,000 in that account."

Explain the role of the court reporter. Advise the client to answer in full sentences so the record will be clear. In that regard, urge the client to be as clear as possible. Point out that if an appeal becomes necessary, the reporter's transcript will reflect all of the testimony and events at the trial so the appellate court can consider any errors. To emphasize the importance of clarity, point out that every word spoken will be taken down by the court reporter and that the client needs to think about the words he or she chooses. Emphasize the need to speak clearly and loud enough for everyone in the courtroom to hear the testimony.

Also remind the client that when nervous (which he or she will be), he or she may talk faster. Remind your client to slow down and speak in a conversational tone rather than racing through testimony. Conversely, the client should be warned about speaking too slowly, making the testimony sound unnatural. Also, if your client tends to mumble, point that out during your rehearsal. Advise the client that mumbling can be perceived as an evasive tactic and that the client's testimony needs to be clear, confident, and forthright.

Assure the client that it is normal to be nervous while testifying. Explain that everyone is nervous, even the professional expert witness. The client should not get down on himself or herself but should harness the nervous energy to do the best job possible. Explain that after a few minutes, he or she will settle down. Reassure your client that you will make sure he or she is well prepared by the time you are done and that he or she will do a great job.

Objections

Advise the client what to do if he or she hears an objection while testifying. Inform your client to immediately stop talking and wait for the judge to rule on the objection. Translate for the client: if the judge *sustains* the objection, the judge considers the objection valid and will instruct the examining attorney to ask another question. Or if the judge *overrules* the objection, the objection is rejected and the judge will instruct the witness to answer the question. Tell the client to listen to the judge's comments and, if he or she has any questions, to ask the judge whether he or she should answer the question. Also, arguments over objections can sometimes be lengthy; advise the client to speak up if he or she doesn't remember the original question asked before the objection.

Oops, I Forgot!

Advise the client that his or her testimony is not a memory test; your client will not be graded on his or her recall. It is normal for people to become forgetful, particularly under pressure. Explain that you can refresh your client's memory by showing him or her something. Walk the client through the procedure:

> "If you say you can't remember something, I will ask you if your memory is exhausted. Say yes if it is. I will then ask you if anything will refresh your memory. If a document or something else will refresh your memory, identify it and then I can show the item to you to look at. But you can't read out loud from it. Read it to yourself and then place it down and answer the question."

Sometimes clients will prepare a cheat sheet to refresh their memory. Remember, the opposing attorney can review any documents used to refresh memory, so make sure the refreshing document doesn't contain information you don't want to share with the opposing party.

Clarify that this recollection procedure can be used either during your examination or during questioning by the other attorney. Assure the client that unless it is an obvious tactic to avoid a question, it will not be held against him or her. Explain to the client that if he or she has continuing memory lapses due to nerves, you can ask for a brief recess. But if the judge denies the request, the client will just need to soldier on.

Direct Examination

In preparing your client for direct examination, give a context. Explain that direct examination is your opportunity to present an important portion of the case through testimony. Describe why direct examination is important, that it is the opportunity for your client to create a human connection with the judge. Discuss broadly the topics that you will cover with the client, giving an overview of the general areas you will cover during direct examination. By giving the client this introduction, it will help him or her relax. Explain that your direct examination will feel like a conversation between the two of you (of course, subject to the opposing lawyer objecting). Urge the client to keep regular eye contact with you throughout the examination.

Remind the client that he or she may only testify to what he or she saw, heard, knows, or remembers; he or she may not guess, speculate, or base testimony on information told to him or her by another. Explain the process of laying a foundation for testimony. Give the client an illustration of how you might lay a foundation for a conversation. Will you admit any exhibits through your client's testimony? If so, show the exhibit to your client and explain the purpose of the exhibit. Explain how you will admit and use the exhibit. If you will need to lay a foundation with the client for its admission, walk him or her through this procedure. Have the client do a mock run-through identifying the exhibit and using the exhibit after you admit it. Explain that he or she may not read from the exhibit until it is admitted into evidence.

Remind the client of the duty to tell the truth: that he or she will be sworn to do so and may not lie. It is important to reinforce the importance of this fact. For the cynical client, explain that not only is it illegal to lie under oath but it is counterproductive as well; the truth has a way of coming out in a trial, and if his or her credibility is questionable on one point, even a small or a collateral point, it will likely be questioned on the important points as well. Explain that if he or she makes a mistake regarding his or her answer, and realizes it after the testimony, he or she should ask to clarify the prior answer as soon as he or she becomes aware of the oversight.

If you have not yet done so, order a copy of the transcript of your client's deposition testimony. Have the client read the transcript and make sure you read it as well. Explain how the opposing attorney can use the deposition transcript and advise the client to remain consistent with his or her answers. If your client needs to veer from earlier testimony, help the client with a strategy for explaining the inconsistency.

Do you anticipate any special problems with the testimony? Will you invoke your client's right to remain silent? Explain to the client the consequences of testifying to a crime or remaining silent. Describe the procedure and help the client decide how to handle the issue. Spend time working through other problems that you will need to explain as part of your case. Advise the client of the need to bring out those problem areas preemptively because the other attorney most certainly will bring them out during cross-examination. Figure out a plausible strategy to explain away your client's weaknesses up front, as opposed to defending them later.

Explain the attorney-client privilege. Remind your client that conversations between the two of you are confidential and that in answering questions—either your questions or those by the opposing counsel—the client shouldn't offer testimony regarding any conversations or discussions between the two of you. Explain the implications of "opening the door" regarding those discussions and why he or she should avoid them during testimony.

Dress Rehearsal

Rehearse the direct examination with the client several times. The first time you rehearse the direct, stop and comment on the client's substantive answers. Suggest alternative ways for the client to answer, but don't specifically tell the client how to answer. Remind the client that he or she must always tell the truth. Discuss and critique his or her answers. Instruct the client regarding delivery: to speak confidently. This exercise will help improve the client's ultimate presentation and help give him or her greater confidence.

If you intend to use exhibits, explain the mechanics of their use in the context of your examination. If you plan on using a demonstrative aid, discuss how you will lay the foundation (that it will help clarify the witness's testimony) and rehearse using the actual exhibit. Make sure the exhibit is correct and the client is comfortable using it.

Remind your client to maintain eye contact with you and not be distracted by his or her spouse chatting to the opposing attorney. Your client should maintain the focus on you throughout the examination. You may want to have the client occasionally look at the judge as well. Sometimes judges are looking down writing notes, but other judges are watching the witness closely. Natural eye contact (as opposed to staged) can be very persuasive. Explain to the client that he or she shouldn't be afraid of looking at the judge if appropriate.

During the second run-through, don't stop. Note problem answers. Pay attention to the client's delivery and body language and log your observations, both with regard to the testimony and the client's demeanor. If possible, have an associate or assistant sit in during this dry run and observe the testimony. Consider having the associate object periodically to help the client practice maintaining composure during objections. Later, ask the associate for any impressions and insights and share those with the client.

At the conclusion of the rehearsal, ask your client questions about the examination. Were there any areas of the examination when he or she felt uncomfortable? Were there any questions that he or she was uncertain about? Think about ways you can respond to your client's concerns and reframe your questions or approach the topics differently. Direct examination is a dance, and you need to watch and listen to your dance partner.

Cross-Examination

All witnesses are terrified of cross-examination; do your best to assuage your client about this unavoidable part of the process. Remind the client of the basic options for his or her testimony: "yes," "no," "I don't know," "I don't understand the question," or "I can't answer the question." Remind the client that it is okay to explain *only* when the question requests an explanation. Tell the client that good cross-examiners rarely offer that opportunity. Explain that one of the goals of the opposing attorney may be to make the client angry and lose composure. Explain that if he or she argues with the examiner, he or she will likely lose both the argument and the sympathy of the judge. Remind the client that when attacked, it is natural to respond defensively, but he or she needs to suppress this very natural impulse. If you describe this in the language of a game, it will be easier for your client to understand. To win the game, the client must maintain composure at all times and not react to the questioning attorney, despite the attorney's best efforts to provoke or irritate. He or she must be cooperative but not a doormat.

Some clients, either because of terror or an obsequious personality, want to please the other attorney, agreeing with everything the lawyer says. If you suspect your client is so inclined, forewarn him or her that he or she is not obliged to agree with everything that comes out of the other attorney's mouth. Point out that good attorneys will get the witness to agree to four or five noncontroversial facts, training the witness to be agreeable, lulling him or her into an admission on a more controversial subject. Make sure the client is conscious of this technique and avoids a mistaken yes. Likewise, tell the client not to be baited by the opposing attorney. Some cross-examiners are very skilled at getting a witness to trip up by a well-timed "oh really" and an arched eyebrow. Advise the client not to take the bait or react to the goad—urge your client to remain calm and steady at all times.

Daniel Small, in his book, discusses the law of the hole. If the client blunders, don't keep trying to fix it; it will become a larger problem. Stop and address the mistake. As Small explains:

> "When you're in a hole, stop digging!" Trying to work around a mistake will ultimately only make it worse. As soon as you realize you made a mistake—however that happens: on your own, because you hear it come back to you in another question, or in some other way—stop and fix it. There are lots of ways to do this, but one of easiest and most effective is the simple word "clarify."[5]

Tell the client that he or she should ask to clarify any earlier mistaken testimony, wrong for whatever reason.

Explain that you will have the opportunity to ask the client clarification questions on redirect examination after the cross-examination is complete. If he or she gets boxed into a yes or no answer that requires an explanation, don't panic. Advise your client to just answer the question as precisely as he or she can, and when you examine again, you will permit him or her to elaborate. Also admonish the client about self-help answers—volunteering explanations beyond the scope of the question. Explain that sometimes witnesses think they are being clever slipping something in, but it usually plays poorly for the judge.

Remind the client that the audience is the judge; it is the judge who the client is trying to influence, not the opposing counsel. Evading or getting into a verbal fistfight with the opposing attorney will not influence the judge favorably. And advise the client not to be cute or

---

5. *Id.* at 83.

sarcastic in his or her demeanor or responses. This is a quick way to lose the game. Essentially the only way the client can win this game against a smart and highly trained adversary is to stay calm, answer the questions to the best of his or her ability, and to wait for the cavalry during redirect.

Sometimes a witness will play chess on the witness stand; when asked a question, his or her mind thinks three chess moves ahead, analyzing the examiner's ultimate goal with the question. Advise the client to avoid doing this; point out that the act of guessing will appear evasive. Just answer, don't analyze the question.

Advise the client that if the opposing attorney's question mischaracterizes earlier testimony or uses loaded words that distort the earlier testimony, answer in the negative. Also advise the client that these types of questions are objectionable and that you will be objecting. Tell the client only to respond to a question positively if it is 100 percent true. If partially incorrect, just answer, "I can't answer that question" or simply "no": "You testified that you always pick up the children from school." If the actual earlier testimony was "I have picked up the children from school," the answer would be "no" as opposed to volunteering the correction.

What Will He or She Ask Me?

Evaluate where your client is weak and consider areas you would hammer if you represented the opposing party. Odds are your opponent will cover much of the same territory, so use that guideline to help the client anticipate. To the extent that you can foresee specific questions, help your client formulate a response during preparation. At the very least, discuss the general areas you expect your opponent to address. And the exercise of anticipating your opponent's questions may help you formulate preemptive questions for your direct examination.

Rehearse the Cross

As you consider your opponent's likely line of cross-examination, draw up an outline for someone to use to rehearse your client. Either use a partner or associate or find a professional friend whom you can call on to cross-examine your client. Critique the examination and point out ways the client can more effectively weather it. Ask your actor to use some sharp elbows during the examination, particularly if your opponent is an aggressive examiner. Often overlooked by lawyers, this exercise will help ease your client's cross anxiety and ultimately increase his or her effectiveness as a witness.

Prepare Other Fact or Lay Opinion Witnesses

Prepare the other witnesses as well. Meet with each witness personally. While you can communicate by phone, a face-to-face meeting is more productive; the witness will be more inclined to ask questions and you will have the opportunity to observe and evaluate the witness's demeanor. While not ideal, if necessary, meet the witness immediately before the trial to review the testimony. Depending upon the importance of the testimony, spend as much time as necessary preparing (but not coaching) the witness. If you intend to admit an exhibit through the witness, explain the authentication process and rehearse its admission. Preparation of a witness called only to lay a foundation for a document will differ from a witness discussing mom's strengths as a parent. Use your judgment on how much time to spend preparing the particular witness. If the witness needs to bring any information, remind him or her to have it at court.

Familiarize the witness with the protocol of the courtroom: instruct him or her on dealing with objections, and help him or her anticipate lines of inquiry on cross. Always remind the witness of the oath to tell the truth. This is not just ethical, it is defensive; if the opposing counsel asks the witness what you told the witness concerning testimony, this will confirm you told him or her to tell the truth, which will enhance both the witness's and your credibility with the court.

Find out whether the witness was contacted by the opposing party, opposing attorney, or investigator. If so, ask the witness to share any information provided. Also, before you call the witness, do your own investigation concerning the witness to anticipate any surprises. Perform an online search and see if anything registers. If it is a professional person, confirm the licensure requirements are met. Ask your client if he or she has a connection with the witness that you should be aware of. If you expect any claims of bias, contemplate ways to soften the claim and bring out the relationship during your direct; don't wait for it to come out on cross.

Coordinate the timing of the witness. Tell the witness where and when he or she will testify. Determine if the witness has any scheduling problems and try to work those out with the opposing attorney. If your opponent does not agree, file a motion for leave to call the witness out of order. If possible, arrange for one of your team to meet the witness immediately before the testimony to answer any last-minute questions.

Prepare Your Expert Witnesses

Typically, the expert witness is more experienced as witnesses; nevertheless, you need to spend more (rather than less) time preparing your expert witness to testify. First discuss your expert's qualifications. If you anticipate a challenge to your expert's qualifications, work with the expert to bolster the credentials. Review the expert's CV with him or her and make sure it is current. Discuss any professional accomplishments left off of the CV. Ask questions regarding education, postgraduate work, publications, etc. Make sure you are fully informed of the expert's achievements.

Even when the opponent doesn't challenge the expertise of the witness, if the case involves competing expert testimony, highlight your expert's achievements when they exceed those of the opposing expert. Remember, you are not obligated to accept the stipulation from your opponent concerning your expert's expertise and are free to reject it in favor of having your expert testify to his accomplishments and expertise. If the expert has been qualified as an expert in prior cases, find out how many times and offer that as part of the qualification phase of the case as well. Rehearse the qualification testimony with the expert, asking the expert to itemize his or her credentials. Make sure you get in the important facts quickly and efficiently.

Discuss the structure of the examination with the expert. Use either a pyramid or an inverted pyramid approach to examining your expert. Under the inverted pyramid approach, you start with the expert's ultimate opinion and work your way down from there, asking questions about how the expert ultimately came to that opinion. Alternatively, you could use the pyramid that starts with the investigation, building up to the ultimate conclusion. Advise the expert how you intend to proceed so he or she has a context.

Walk the expert through your outline and discuss the important parts of his or her testimony. Much of this should have been done before deposition testimony, but a refresher is a good idea. Also, you can discuss problems that arose during deposition and attempt to remedy those during direct examination. If your witness has testified before and knows the basic rules of testifying, a brief discussion of how to handle objections, questions from the opposing counsel, and courtroom protocol will suffice. If the expert has never testified before, you will need to review these topics more exhaustively.

Help the expert anticipate cross-examination. Prior to meeting with the expert, review his or her deposition testimony and the questions asked. What would you ask the expert if you were crossing him or her? Discuss any issues of bias based upon the expert's prior work for you or your firm. Remind the expert to be forthcoming, if he or she has done prior work for you, and to not be defensive or evasive. Discuss with the expert where he or she perceives his or her report may have chinks in the armor. Where might it be exposed? Help the expert anticipate questions dealing with those shortcomings and develop realistic strategies for dealing with them.

Advise your expert that hypothetical questions from the opposing counsel may be asked. Remind your expert that if he or she legitimately can't answer a question that it's okay to say so. On the other hand, if a fair question is asked and the expert tries to dodge it, he or she will look evasive, affecting his or her overall credibility. Explain that based upon the hypothetical, he or she will likely be forced to concede certain things. If the expert becomes an advocate, or tries too hard to support an unsupportable position, he or she loses much of his or her authority as an expert. Educate your expert regarding the "law of the hole" and urge him or her to stop digging if he or she ends up in one. Remind your expert that you will be able to examine him or her after the opposing attorney and that you will allow him or her to explain a position. Tell your expert that sometimes he or she may need to concede certain issues to salvage his or her expertise as a whole.

Typically experts are very smart. Advise the expert not to be imperious or snarky, lose his or her cool, or argue with the opposing attorney; that type of behavior is the kiss of death for credibility. Tell the expert that it is natural to become condescending when challenged—prompt him or her to keep that impulse in check and gracefully respond to the taunts as best he or she can. Advise your expert that the best way to defeat an aggressive opponent is by keeping calm and focusing on answering the questions to the best of his or her ability.

Review

You are almost there. Just as you invested time early to think about your proofs, take the time now to think about your case organically, how all of the pieces will be put together shortly. Draft, refine, and polish your opening statement and closing argument. Take the time to think about their content and structure. Do they make sense? Is your presentation persuasive or just background noise? You have the time to invest, so use it wisely. There is no excuse not to prepare your client and other witnesses for the trial. The excuse for most lawyers is lack of time in the crazy days leading up to the trial, but that doesn't apply when you start early. Use your last month—not your last week—to get ready. In the next chapter, I will discuss what you should be doing during your last week.

30-Day Checklist

- ☐ Prepare trial memorandum.
  - ☐ legal research
  - ☐ summary of the issues in dispute
  - ☐ summary of noncontroversial/undisputed facts
  - ☐ summary of witnesses disclosed by both parties
  - ☐ proposed exhibit list
  - ☐ any stipulations already reached or sought
- ☐ Prepare opening statement.
  - ☐ brainstorm grabber
  - ☐ outline
  - ☐ include references to theory and themes
  - ☐ rehearse
- ☐ Prepare closing argument.
  - ☐ written or oral?
  - ☐ include facts, law, and emotion
  - ☐ rehearse
- ☐ Will demonstrative aids help opening or closing?
  - ☐ how to use
  - ☐ when to use
  - ☐ formats (poster board, projection, PowerPoint, etc.)
  - ☐ prepare rough draft of demonstrative
  - ☐ finalize demonstrative aid
- ☐ Consider final pretrial motions.
  - ☐ motion in limine to bar cumulative testimony
  - ☐ motion to bar evidence or issues not properly disclosed
  - ☐ motion to pare down witness list
  - ☐ motion to have the admissibility of prospective evidence ruled on in advance
  - ☐ motion to determine anticipated claims of privilege
  - ☐ motion to take judicial notice of certain evidence
  - ☐ motion for leave to call a witness out of order

- ☐ motion to bar witnesses from observing other witness testimony
- ☐ motion to allow an expert witness to observe opposing expert's testimony

☐ Prepare for final pretrial. Use the conference to do the following:

- ☐ solicit stipulations
- ☐ address evidentiary issues
- ☐ schedule witnesses

☐ Have exhibits been exchanged?

☐ Have you reviewed opposing party's proposed exhibits?

☐ Discuss with judge preferences with exhibits.

☐ Request necessary accommodations for client.

☐ Discuss settlement.

☐ Have all witnesses been confirmed?

☐ Are appointments set for preparation?

☐ Use client meeting to discuss the following:

- ☐ trial procedure
- ☐ format of testimony
- ☐ rules regarding objections
- ☐ possibility of being called as an adverse witness
- ☐ set up follow-up meeting with client to rehearse the direct examination

Other Witness Preparation

☐ Schedule preparation conferences.

☐ Discuss wardrobe and demeanor.

☐ Discuss trial procedure and protocol.

☐ Conduct a field trip to courthouse.

☐ Explain lawyer's role at trial.

☐ Confirm date, location, and time of testimony.

☐ Confirm where and who to meet at courthouse.

☐ Explain procedure and objections.

☐ Explain the role of the court reporter, bailiff, judge, etc.

- ☐ Order translator (if applicable).
- ☐ Provide rules of effective testimony.
    - ☐ speak loud and clear
    - ☐ moderate pace
    - ☐ listen, pause, and then answer
    - ☐ don't guess
    - ☐ what to do if you hear an objection
    - ☐ procedure for forgetfulness
- ☐ Discuss witnesses' direct examination.
    - ☐ overview of topics
    - ☐ procedure for foundations
    - ☐ rectifying mistakes
    - ☐ tell the truth
    - ☐ Fifth Amendment issues?
    - ☐ privilege issues
- ☐ Schedule a dress rehearsal for direct examination/cross-examination.
- ☐ Would a demonstrative aid enhance testimony?
    - ☐ If so, prepare the exhibit.
    - ☐ Explain how to use to client.
    - ☐ Format? (poster board, projector, whiteboard, etc.)
- ☐ Discuss expected cross-examination with the witness.
    - ☐ Answer only the question asked.
    - ☐ Don't argue.
    - ☐ Don't volunteer information.
    - ☐ Don't guess.
    - ☐ Think about the question.
    - ☐ The opposing lawyer is not your friend; don't agree to everything.
    - ☐ Correct mistakes.
    - ☐ Cover likely topics.
    - ☐ Any problems from the deposition to cure?

  - ☐ Remember: you will have an opportunity to redirect witness.
- ☐ Conduct a dress rehearsal.
  - ☐ Find associate or other lawyer to conduct.
  - ☐ Deconstruct with witness.
- ☐ Prepare the expert.
  - ☐ Discuss appropriate demeanor and tone.
  - ☐ Get transcript from the deposition.
  - ☐ Discuss problem areas.
  - ☐ Make sure the CV is updated.
  - ☐ Discuss how you will use demonstrative exhibits.
  - ☐ Review the structure of your direct examination.
  - ☐ Discuss how to handle himself or herself on cross.
  - ☐ Discuss topics likely to be covered on cross.
  - ☐ Discuss the procedure for hypotheticals.

CHAPTER 5
7 Days Before Trial

Whoever is first in the field and awaits the coming of the enemy, will be fresh for the fight; whoever is second in the field and has to hasten to battle will arrive exhausted.

—Sun Tzu, *The Art of War*

Introduction

Assuming the prescriptions in this book have been followed, the week before the trial should be used for tweaking, refining, and most importantly, relaxing. You are ready and probably have some silent satisfaction knowing your opponent is scrambling to do things you completed weeks ago. Use this last-minute time for pushing pebbles rather than moving boulders. Handle the last-minute details arising from your upcoming commitment and organize things so that you minimize those unnecessary surprises at trial.

Look at Your Calendar

Look at your calendar and action list over the coming week. Is there anything that you prefer to avoid in light of the upcoming trial? Or alternatively, are there things you want to get out of the way before fully committing yourself to the trial? And don't forget your personal life. Are there events that you have scheduled that you may want to rethink on the eve of trial? While now is not the time to realize that you are scheduled to be on vacation the day the trial commences, sometimes things happen! Ask yourself whether you really want to attend that party the night before the trial is set to commence. Address any scheduling conflicts immediately or make alternative plans.

Make sure you will be free immediately at the end of the trial day, and don't commit yourself to any appointments or commitments. You will be both hyped up and exhausted, and it is not the time to be conducting new client interviews. Instead, at the end of each day, reflect on the testimony; prepare a memorandum summarizing important points that you may want to address later in the trial or at closing argument. Use after-trial time to reorganize yourself: Make sure your exhibit list is current and loose papers have been put in the appropriate place. Plan for the next day or otherwise remain focused on the trial rather than trying to catch up on other client matters.

Consider if you have any tasks that can be delegated rather than worrying about late nights trying to get everything done. Not unlike leaving to go on vacation for a few days, many loose ends that need to get done seem to spring up on the eve of a trial. Focus is critical at this point, and spreading yourself too thin will exhaust you at a time when you need to consolidate your energy. Pass down the line tasks that you don't need to personally perform, freeing up both time and energy.

Address Fees

For the third time, I bring up this subject. Don't ignore it! Has your client paid as agreed? Is the client using the same diligence to pay you that you have used in preparing for this trial? While it is probably too late to withdraw from the case if the client has not paid as agreed, a polite (or not so polite) reminder is in order at this point. Hopefully you have monitored the client's compliance earlier so there are no last-minute hard feelings.

Conduct Final Settlement Discussions

It is not unusual for people to get serious about settlement on the eve of trial. Don't settle now because of a lack of nerve; settle only if it makes sense to your client in light of the total circumstances (particularly now that the client has committed thousands of dollars to trial preparation). Look at your earlier notes reflecting your client's goals and objectives and consider any last-minute offers in light of those goals.

Again, you are ready to go. You don't need to grovel for a settlement offer. In fact, the most likely way to receive such an offer is to quietly prepare for trial and wait. Focus on being superbly ready and you will be amazed by how many proposals find their way to you. Sometimes you may believe an offer meets or exceeds what you expect from a verdict. Advise the client, both orally and in writing. Some people, emotionally invested in proceeding, will demand to forge ahead. Don't make yourself crazy demanding that they settle. All you can do is all you can do—if you fully admonish them of the risks of proceeding (both orally and in writing), they assume that responsibility, not you. In the event the verdict is unsatisfactory, you will have the necessary backup if the client tries to lay blame at your doorstep.

Coordinate Your Team

Who (if anyone) is coming with you to trial? If you intend to use a trial assistant, notify him or her of the exact responsibilities. "You will be coming with me" is not good enough. Consider using trial assistants in the following manner:

- taking detailed notes so you can concentrate on the testimony
- keeping track of the exhibits
- greeting witnesses while the trial is in progress
- managing client needs, freeing you up to concentrate on other tasks
- organizing the file as the case progresses

Does your case consist of boxes of documents? Can you use an assistant to haul everything to the courthouse and set you up each day? Keeping in mind Frank Lloyd Wright's admonishment to his assistant, "an architect always carries his own drawings," perhaps having an assistant set you up and break you down each day will relieve some of the wear and tear, allowing you to better focus on the real task at hand. And despite being superbly prepared, anticipate the unexpected. You may possibly forget something. Make sure that someone is available to make a delivery if necessary.

Will an associate or partner be examining any witnesses or handling any distinct parts of the trial? Make sure to monitor his or her preparation and double-check his or her readiness. If this is your case, you are ultimately responsible. A quick check-in is warranted to make sure there is no confusion or questions.

And don't forget the office front. Provide specific directions to those not attending the trial on how to address issues that arise while you are concentrating on the trial. Do you want a daily memo of calls and other activity or contemporaneous e-mails? Appoint a designated hitter to handle your phone calls in your absence. Advise your assistant what to say to clients when they call in and ask to speak with you. You owe it to the client to concentrate fully on the trial to the extent possible. Develop an action plan to delegate, deal with, or defer other client issues until the conclusion of the trial.

Many of us receive hundreds of e-mails daily. One of the byproducts of the digital age is that people expect responses immediately. Again, either assign a staff member to review your incoming e-mail and take the necessary action, or use an out-of-office feature on your e-mail to advise people that you are engaged in a trial and not able to respond immediately. Redirect them to your assistant or another attorney in the office.

A sole practitioner has unique challenges as a result of the lack of a support staff. Solos need to be creative in addressing other clients' issues without formal staff backup. Consider a digital assistant for the period of the trial. Or blast an e-mail to other clients notifying them of your temporary absence and providing your cell number for emergencies. In any event, the point here is to think of ways to free yourself from the daily demands of the practice to concentrate and focus on the immediate task before you.

Practice More Visualization

In chapter 1, I discussed visualization as a tool to organize your proofs. Now use it to plan some of the details. Pause and think about some of the following details to both plan and mentally prepare:

- What time will the trial start and end?
- When will I leave to go to court?
- Will a court reporter be present or do I need to hire one?
- How will I get to the courthouse (drive, walk, cab, etc.)?
- What time will I be able to set up?
- Will I need the help of an assistant to set up?
- Will it proceed in consecutive days or over a period of time?
- Where will I eat lunch?

- Do I need cash or change for copiers?
- Do I need a haircut, manicure, or shoeshine?
- What will I wear to the trial?
- Do I need to take anything to the dry cleaners, or is my wardrobe ready?

You want to look and feel your best, and anticipating some of these smaller details will help you feel good and smooth your transition into trial. You will feel more confident if trivial issues can be planned in advance. On the day of trial, concentrate your energy on the trial itself, not where you will have lunch.

Practice, Practice, Practice

Set aside time to rehearse your opening statement and closing argument. Again, if you cannot make the presentations purely from memory, rely only on notes and don't read from a script. If you want to start by writing out these important monologues, do so, but in your various practice sessions, continue to reduce them to bare-bones prompts, ultimately memorizing them if possible. Great trial lawyers learn how to memorize presentations, which enhances their credibility and effectiveness as advocates.[1]

Find Systems for Note Taking

How will you keep track of everything as it occurs? Will you use legal pads with multiple colored pens or have you developed some hieroglyphic way of keeping track of information during your note taking. Do you intend to take verbatim notes or abbreviated reminders? Much of this is personal to the lawyer, but you should be conscious of how you intend to keep track of information while things unfold at the trial.

Personally, I never take notes at trial and bring an assistant, who takes detailed notes. I focus my attention on observing and thinking rather than recording. At the end of each day, the assistant prepares a memorandum summarizing the key points of the testimony, and

1. Read *Moonwalking with Einstein: The Art and Science of Remembering Everything* by Joshua Foer (2011), a book that discusses strategies that mentalists and gold-medal memory experts use to memorize large amounts of data.

I personally prepare a separate memo that is more impressionistic, focused on observations I have made during the day. I only keep notes of information that I intend to specifically use in prospective witness examinations. I use different colored pens for notes I intend to ask different witnesses. With regard to important information that I want to emphasize in my closing argument, I bring index cards and write the important fact or impression on the index cards and then incorporate those items into the closing argument.

Pack for Court

Pack for court several days before trial. Early packing serves two purposes. First, early packing allows you the mental space to think about what you need rather than scurrying around the office last minute. Second, early packing serves the psychological purpose of allowing you space to relax before the battle. Get the file put together and put it away to allow you to not think about it for a few days. Your creativity and energy will increase if you can pause for a few days before starting.

Besides your trial notebook, what else do you need to have? Consider the following:

- all evidentiary exhibits organized and collated
- copies of exhibit lists to keep track of all exhibits admitted, both yours and the adverse party's
- copies of exhibits for the judge and opposing counsel
- any demonstrative exhibits
- cell phone with power cord
- laptop and power cords
- small portable printer
- batteries
- electrical tape
- projectors
- laser pointer
- whiteboards or flip chart and markers
- easels
- extension cords
- note pads or legal pads
- index cards
- sticky notes

- extra note pad and pens for the client
- pens and highlighters (multiple colors)
- paper clips or staplers
- extra file folders
- reference materials (dictionary,[2] evidence book, statute)
- personal items (extra hearing-aid batteries, glasses, lens cloth, mints, etc.)
- water and energy drinks
- energy snacks or fruit

Some lawyers bring their entire client file, usually because they think they might need something that was unplanned for. First, if you plan well, you should anticipate the specific things you will need and have them incorporated into your trial notebook. But beyond that, your energy and mental focus disperse if you surround yourself with boxes of unnecessary paper.

Sometimes lawyers haul nearly a dozen banker's boxes into the courtroom to show they *really* mean business. Don't be psyched out. In truth, rather than suggesting strength or gravitas, this display usually indicates lack of good preparation. That being said: always expect the unexpected, and better to have too much than regret not having that critical item you didn't anticipate needing. But in the digital era, you can have the security of having your entire file on your laptop without hauling unnecessary boxes to bolster your self-confidence.

Ask: What About the Client?

Check in with the client a few days before the trial. Remind your client about the time and date and see if he or she has any last-minute questions. Reassure the client and give a pep talk to help your client mentally cope with this difficult pregame time.

My firm has developed a client survival box that we give to clients on the first day of trial. It is lighthearted and designed to help the client relax. In the box we include chocolate, a book of affirming quotes, aspirin, a stress-reduction ball, and other little items to loosen things up. Consider preparing such a gift to help your clients and remind them that you are thinking about them.

---

2. Sometimes a witness plays games with definitions, and it is handy to have a dictionary on hand.

Double-Check Technology and Props

If your presentation is heavily dependent on technology, double-check to make sure everything is working properly. Do you have the know-how to fluidly and quickly use the technology? Consider using an assistant who is more skilled at using the technology so you don't have to think about it or fumble around with it in the middle of the trial. Nothing is more detrimental to your presentation (and confidence) than to have a critical aspect of your case depend on technology and discover that it doesn't work! Self-knowledge includes knowing your limitations; don't depend on technology if you are not adept at it.

What will be available at court? Determine in advance whether the court has a projector or whether you will need to bring one. Likewise, are there whiteboards or easels available? Make sure to see what is available before bringing your own.

Ask the judge at the final pretrial of the possibility of you or an assistant setting up early. Make sure the outlets are located to allow easy plug-in. If not, bring extension cords with electrical tape to tape up the cords so nobody trips. After you set up, do a dry run to test everything. Check and double-check: have everything set to go at the commencement of the trial to save time, aggravation, and potential embarrassment.

Perform One Last Check

One last check is in order. Consult the comprehensive checklist in the appendix of this book. Make sure nothing registers with you as incomplete or undone. While it may be too late to cure certain omissions, better to know now than to be surprised tomorrow.

Develop Rituals

Professional athletes rely on rituals, and so should trial lawyers. Develop personal rituals as a way to reduce anxiety, increase confidence, and enhance performance. Psychologists have confirmed that what appear to be superstitions actually help anchor us and improve performance. And for peak performers, rituals developed over years become second nature. Tennis great Rafael Nadal undertakes a series of rituals before every serve in order to help him focus and relax. Are there rituals you could adopt? Maybe you have a lucky tie or eat the same things on trial days.[3] Whatever the ritual, make sure you consistently rely on it as part of your routine.

Relax

One of the most beneficial and overlooked aspects of peak performance is making sure you are relaxed. All of the suggestions leading up to this point are designed to promote maximum relaxation on the eve of trial. Get a massage, exercise, take some walks, or make some time to meditate: breathe and unwind. All of the martial arts emphasize the importance of relaxation as a way to focus your personal energy. When you are mentally tight, your ability to think effectively is compromised. Your last day or two should remain focused on relaxation and mental focus.

Sleep is vital to effective functioning. Go to bed early enough to get enough sleep. The night before the trial, make sure to engage in good-sleep-inducing behavior (although in all honesty, I don't think I have ever slept great the night before a trial).

And along the same line, stay positive. Engage in only positive self-talk and do not disparage yourself, no matter how insecure you may feel. Develop positive affirmations for yourself and review them multiple times in the days leading up to the trial. Some affirmations to consider:

- I feel strong and powerful, happy and energetic.
- I love trying cases.
- My ability to conquer my challenges is limitless; my potential to succeed is infinite.
- I am a winner.
- There is always a solution as long as I stay calm and think.
- I know I can do this.
- I am a warrior, not a worrier.
- I meet every situation knowing I am its master.
- I am calm and confident regardless of what happens.

3. I once ate two hard-boiled eggs for lunch every day during a 20-day trial.

Positive affirmations will seep into your unconscious mind if repeated regularly with emotional energy. Believe what you are saying, and these positive statements will increase your confidence and enhance your performance. Use them, particularly when you are feeling unsteady or uncertain about yourself.

Review

Seven days is simultaneously an eternity and a blink of an eye on the eve of an important event. Use the time wisely and don't panic. Stay strong: you have been planning for this event for months and are ready to go. Make it happen—don't lose courage and go flat now. Trust yourself and your preparation. All of your checklists have been consulted, and you have done everything humanly possible to help your client achieve his or her goal. Congratulate yourself, not necessarily on the end result, but on your self-discipline and focus over the past several months. Focus on your positives and what you have accomplished rather than your faults and what you could have done better. "You can do it!"

7-Day Checklist

- ☐ Review your calendar.
  - ☐ Any conflicts?
  - ☐ Anything need to be rescheduled?
  - ☐ Have I set aside time after court to deconstruct the day?
  - ☐ Anything I should delegate?

Receivable Review

- ☐ Any settlement offers to review or discuss with your client?
- ☐ Coordinate the team.
  - ☐ Who will accompany you to trial?
  - ☐ Have you instructed that person?
  - ☐ Will someone set up and break down each day?
  - ☐ Will you use a technology assistant?
  - ☐ Can you get in early to set up?
  - ☐ Have you notified your assistant how to update you with daily developments?
  - ☐ Who will take your phone calls?
  - ☐ Set up an out-of-office e-mail assistant.
  - ☐ Who is lined up to handle emergencies?
  - ☐ Is someone available to make courthouse deliveries?

Miscellaneous Considerations

- ☐ How will you get to court?
- ☐ What time will you leave to go to court?
- ☐ Where will you have lunch?
- ☐ Will you need cash or change?
- ☐ Is your wardrobe determined?
- ☐ Personal grooming:
  - ☐ hair
  - ☐ nails
  - ☐ laundry or dry cleaning
  - ☐ shoeshine

- ☐ Practice opening and closing.
- ☐ Pack
  - ☐ trial notebook
  - ☐ copies of your exhibits with exhibit list
  - ☐ copies of opponent's exhibits with exhibit list
  - ☐ demonstrative exhibits with copy for court record
  - ☐ cell phone and power cord
  - ☐ laptop with power cord
  - ☐ electrical tape
  - ☐ projector
  - ☐ whiteboard
  - ☐ flip chart
  - ☐ markers
  - ☐ easels
  - ☐ extension cords
  - ☐ legal pads
  - ☐ index cards
  - ☐ sticky notes or flags
  - ☐ extra notepad for the client
  - ☐ pens and highlighters
  - ☐ paper clips or staplers
  - ☐ file folders
  - ☐ dictionary
  - ☐ evidence reference book
  - ☐ statute or code of procedure
  - ☐ personal items (glasses, lens cloth, hearing-aid battery)
  - ☐ water
  - ☐ energy drinks
  - ☐ energy snacks

- ☐ Download file to laptop.
- ☐ Check in with client.
- ☐ Prepare trial survival package.
- ☐ Double-check technology.
- ☐ Repeat positive affirmations.
- ☐ Relax!

CHAPTER 6
Concluding the Case

The credit belongs to the man who is actually in the arena, whose face is marred by dust and sweat and blood; who strives valiantly; who errs, who comes short again and again, because there is no effort without error and shortcoming; but who does actually strive to do the deeds; who knows great enthusiasms, the great devotions; who spends himself in a worthy cause; who at the best knows in the end the triumph of high achievement, and who at the worst, if he fails, at least fails while daring greatly, so that his place shall never be with those cold and timid souls who neither know victory nor defeat.

—Theodore Roosevelt

Introduction

Congratulations on completing your case. Regardless of the judge's ruling, if you were prepared, patient, and purposeful, you succeeded. In a divorce trial, you are not only testing your choice of legal theory and presentation, you are also testing yourself. And by finishing the case (presumably still standing!), you have passed the test. If things didn't come out the way you wanted, analyze the loss. What could you have done better? If you screwed something up, acknowledge it and learn from it, but ultimately you need to let it go. Nobody is perfect, and much is out of our control. Accept your flaws with grace and humility and move on.

Discuss the Result with the Client

After the court rules, sit down with the client and discuss the ruling. Often, courts will take the matter under advisement. Good or bad, notify the client immediately when the ruling comes in. It is critical that you drop everything to notify the client, particularly when the ruling is less than hoped for. The last thing you want is for your client's spouse to notify your client with a gloating phone call.

Schedule a time to meet with the client to discuss the ruling, answer questions, and advise the client of the procedural next steps. While you may be exhausted and burned out on the case, don't just send a letter enclosing a copy of the ruling. A face-to-face meeting helps ease the client's anxiety and also helps maintain the client's confidence in you, particularly when he or she is disappointed in the ruling.

Follow up the ruling with a letter confirming all of the client's options: post-trial motions, appeal, etc. If the ruling reserved any issues or otherwise requires follow-up by the attorneys, make sure to explain to the client what that entails. For example, a ruling dividing a retirement plan requires the preparation and processing of a qualified domestic relations order (QDRO). Don't let this follow-up fall off of your radar. Make sure to prepare all necessary transfer documents or other documents necessary to finish the case. It is not unusual, particularly after you have been neglecting most of your other cases for the past several weeks, to put off these routine cleanup tasks, but if they are not done immediately, they may become problems in the future by virtue of their neglect. Abraham Lincoln observed that diligence should be the leading rule for lawyers: "Leave nothing for tomorrow, which can be done today." Analyze the ruling for necessary follow-up by you, make a to-do list, and diligently follow up with all of your tasks necessary to complete the matter.

At the end of the case, you may have a large balance due. While it may be a sore subject, particularly if it is an unsatisfactory ruling, don't ignore it. Discuss the client's options and terms of payment. Lawyers sometimes assume responsibility because of a bad ruling and pay penance by forgoing fees. Or alternatively, they attempt to appease an angry client by writing off the balance. This is why I advised you to make sure the fees are paid in advance of the trial; by doing so, you don't have to address this difficult issue. But if the fees are earned, either make arrangements at this time or consider options to collect the outstanding fees.

Explain Appeals and Post-Trial Motions

Make sure to confirm with the client, again in writing, the time sensitivity of the decision to file post-trial motions or appeals. Don't take for granted that the client knows there is a limited period of time to invoke his or her right to appeal. If the client advises you that he or she is done and does not want to appeal, confirm that fact but remind your client that his or her spouse can appeal regardless.

Explain that an appeal is legally separate from the trial and requires a new engagement agreement. Discuss the approximate cost of prosecuting or defending an appeal, including the costs of transcripts. If the client has a balance due, explain that the trial fees need to be resolved before you agree to accept the new assignment. If you choose to no longer represent the client, consider referring him or her to an appellate attorney. Regardless of whether you refer the client or not, clearly confirm in writing that you will not take any further action on behalf of the client.

Put a Bow on It

Marketers often talk about the importance of first impressions when lawyers meet a new client. But just as important is the last impression—how you leave things after you have completed the case. Tell the client (if it's true) how much you admire his or her grace and fortitude during the difficult months of the divorce. Clients should not only be admonished when they misbehave during a case, they should also be commended on their good behavior. We have all seen people who have been near heroic in their stoicism and patience, and these people should be acknowledged. Help the client move forward with his or her life. Encourage the client to let go of the divorce and focus on the future and rebuilding his or her life. Explain that some people tragically never get over the divorce and that you hope for more from the client. A pep talk about a positive future helps conclude your relationship in a positive way.

In certain cases, it may be appropriate to have a party to recognize the client. Consider having an informal get-together at the office or off campus and celebrating the conclusion of the case with the client. Over the course of time, the client may have gotten close with you and your staff, and a party is a good way to say bon voyage into the client's new life.

Refer the client to other professionals. Give the client names of an estate-planning attorney, an accountant, a financial planner, a therapist, or others who you think might help the client. Explain how these professionals may be able to help the client. For example, advise the client that it may be a good time to prepare a new estate plan or reconsider his or her tax withholding. Provide the client a specific punch list of things to think about or do to tie up any loose ends.

Ask for an honest review of yourself. What could you have done differently to help make the process better? Sometimes it is difficult to hear your faults, but it is necessary for growth. Solicit a critique of you and your staff. Use the insights from the client to help improve your systems and future case management. Constant and never-ending improvement should be the mantra of all professionals.

Purge the File

Purge the file of excess copies and other unnecessary documents. Paper seems to accumulate throughout the trial, so at the conclusion of the case, take the time to organize it. With regard to the trial file and all exhibits, keep everything intact until post-trial motions are resolved. After the case is done, however, there is no need to keep everything. Storage space is always limited, and if you already have everything stored digitally, you don't need to keep the boxes of paper created for the trial. If there are original documents that belong to the client, pull those and return them to the client, but most records (already digitally stored on your hard drive) can be shredded at the conclusion of the case.

Acknowledge the People Involved

Make sure to acknowledge those persons who helped you on your journey. Send notes to your experts or other witnesses regarding the ruling and any pertinent comments made by the judge. Expert witnesses, in particular, love to hear how the judge received their testimony or analysis, and a brief note describing your impressions is a great way to engender goodwill with the expert. If others assisted, consider writing a note to them as well. For example, if a copy service assisted you in preparing exhibits, send them a thank-you note or acknowledge them somehow. At my firm, we send a box of chocolates to those witnesses or others who helped us during the case. Always remember to show your gratitude to people who help you.

Take Up Journaling

Get out of the office and spend some quiet time thinking about the case and the recent ruling. Reflect on all of the events leading up to the conclusion of the case. Consider some of the following:

- What trial strategies worked well?
- What strategies didn't work?
- If you had the case to try again, what would you do differently?
- Knowing what you know now, how would you have prepared differently?
- How would you have better managed your relationship with your client?
- How could you have more effectively used your team?

Keeping a professional journal is a way to document your professional growth and serves as a resource for future challenges that you may confront. Trial lawyers are inherently lifelong learners, and a central place to store all of the lessons along the way is indispensable.

Review

At the conclusion of a journey, you are often exhausted and ready to move on. A trial is a type of journey, but your work is not done yet. Help the client ease into his or her new life by counseling and coaching. While the result doesn't impact you personally, empathize and help the client accept it. Don't be defensive or try to distract the client by describing an obvious disappointment as a positive. Have the integrity to stand with the client while he or she absorbs the impact of the ruling. On the other hand, celebrate with the client when appropriate; share your client's joy and urge the client to accept his or her good fortune magnanimously.

The courtroom is your classroom. Reflect on your professional endeavors and evaluate them. The education of a trial lawyer is a process; learn from each experience and grow as you progress through your career. Excellence has no ultimate destination; it is the road to it that matters.

Concluding the Case Checklist

- ☐ Review the ruling.
- ☐ Prepare a checklist with all follow-up tasks to complete:
  - ☐ Execute deeds.
  - ☐ Prepare title transfers or assignments: stock, vehicles, etc.
  - ☐ Do QDROs or transfer of retirement need to be done?
  - ☐ Any accounting necessary to implement judgment?
  - ☐ Deadlines for post-trial motions or appeal docketed?
  - ☐ Necessity of support withholding orders?
- ☐ Meet with the client to discuss the ruling:
  - ☐ advise of implications of ruling
  - ☐ next steps/options concerning post-trial motions or appeal
  - ☐ tax implications of ruling/divorce
  - ☐ changing estate plan
  - ☐ cancellation of joint debt
  - ☐ significant future dates
  - ☐ implications of noncompliance with court order
  - ☐ procedure for future modification (and what can be modified)
  - ☐ arrangements regarding outstanding fees
- ☐ Send letter to client confirming options and obligations.
- ☐ Throw a party for client?
- ☐ Purge the file.
  - ☐ Return originals to client.
  - ☐ Shred duplicates.
- ☐ Send thank-you notes/acknowledgments
- ☐ Keep a journal.

Appendix
The Checklists

100-Day Checklist

- ☐ Read the entire case file.
- ☐ Read the statute, case law, and secondary materials.
- ☐ Prepare a case notebook.
- ☐ Diary any critical dates and reminders 14 days, 7 days, and 1day before the deadline.
- ☐ Prepare an outcome narrative.
- ☐ Prepare a statement summarizing the theory of the case.
- ☐ What is the theme of the case?
- ☐ What grabbers will summarize the theme?
- ☐ Prepare a narrative summarizing the desired outcome of the case.
- ☐ Perform a trial visualization exercise.
- ☐ Use the madman-architect-builder-judge exercise.
- ☐ Prepare a mind map of the case.
- ☐ Perform a critical analysis of the opponent's case.
- ☐ Prepare proposed findings of fact and judgment.
- ☐ Prepare a preliminary proof chart.
- ☐ Conduct an organizational team meeting.
- ☐ Block out weekly time between now and the trial.
- ☐ Create a notebook dedicated to preparation prompts.
- ☐ Discuss fees with the client.
- ☐ Confirm fee agreement in writing.
- ☐ Diary fee-compliance review.

90-Day Checklist

- ☐ Diary all deadlines with 14-, 7-, and 1-day reminders.
- ☐ If not already set by court order or court rule, request that the court set deadlines for the following (where appropriate):
  - ☐ completion of initial written discovery
  - ☐ completion of supplemental written discovery
  - ☐ disclosure of all witnesses
  - ☐ disclosure of substance of witness testimony and/or opinions
  - ☐ completion of depositions
  - ☐ production of expert reports/opinions
  - ☐ production of rebuttal or surebutter expert reports/opinions
  - ☐ exchange of exhibits
- ☐ Do you have all of the data necessary to support your theory and theme?
- ☐ If not, what is the most efficient way to obtain the information?
- ☐ Conduct a general discovery audit.
  - ☐ Have you complied with all written discovery requests?
  - ☐ Do you owe any updates to previously answered discovery?
  - ☐ Have you timely filed formal objections to improper requests?
  - ☐ Have you scheduled any objections for hearing?
  - ☐ Have you disclosed all witnesses in writing?
  - ☐ Has the opposing party disclosed witnesses?
  - ☐ Does the opposing party owe any discovery responses?
  - ☐ Do you need any updates to prior discovery responses?
  - ☐ Have you requested answers or updates?
  - ☐ Have you sent a letter to resolve differences concerning deficiencies?
- ☐ Is a motion to compel production of discovery or disclosures appropriate or necessary?

- ☐ Do you need to depose anyone?
- ☐ Have depositions been scheduled?
- ☐ Is an order to compel depositions necessary?

Discovery Compliance

- ☐ Diary all deadlines with ticklers.
- ☐ Meet with client to allocate responsibility for answers/production.
- ☐ Review client answers.
- ☐ Bates-stamp and scan completed production.
- ☐ Serve responses on opposing attorney.

Experts

- ☐ Do you need an expert for
  - ☐ valuation of real estate?
  - ☐ business valuation?
  - ☐ appraisal of personal property?
  - ☐ classification of assets?
  - ☐ tracing contributions of nonmarital property?
  - ☐ proving income?
  - ☐ proving lifestyle?
  - ☐ tax issues?
  - ☐ educating the court on a complex topic?
  - ☐ child development?
  - ☐ child custody?
- ☐ Have you investigated any potential expert?
  - ☐ If unknown, have you consulted references?
  - ☐ Have you reviewed the potential expert's CV?
  - ☐ Have you reviewed the expert's publications?
  - ☐ Have you personally interviewed the expert?
  - ☐ Have you determined the potential expert's fees?
- ☐ Have you consulted the client about hiring the expert?
- ☐ Do you have an engagement agreement with the expert?

- ☐ Are all disclosure dates known and noted in the diary?
- ☐ Have you prepared a letter to the client confirming the decision to hire (or not) an expert for the case?
- ☐ Have payment arrangements with the expert been made?
- ☐ Has the client paid the expert, or do you have an advance from the client to do so?
- ☐ Has your expert been notified of all deadlines in writing?
- ☐ Has your expert report been produced to the opposing party?
- ☐ Have you received the adverse expert's report?
- ☐ Have you received the adverse expert's CV?
- ☐ Have you investigated the adverse expert's credentials and/or publications?
- ☐ Will you challenge the expertise of the opposing expert?
- ☐ Are there any aspects of the opposing expert report that are subject to a *Daubert* challenge?
- ☐ Have you set up a meeting with your expert to review the adverse party report?
- ☐ Have you set the deposition of the adverse expert (or decided not to depose the expert)?
- ☐ Do you have to pay the adverse expert for his or her time? If so, have arrangements been made?
- ☐ Have you set up a meeting to prepare your expert for deposition?

Property

- ☐ Has a marital balance sheet been prepared?
- ☐ Have you prepared a discrete notebook or folder for the property?
- ☐ Have all assets been valued?
- ☐ How will you prove asset values?
- ☐ Have you solicited stipulations concerning asset values?
- ☐ Have all valuation experts/reports been disclosed?
- ☐ Are there any claims of dissipation or waste?
- ☐ Have you provided necessary notice to the opposing party?
- ☐ Do you have any asset classification issues?

- ☐ Have you determined your theory regarding asset classification?
- ☐ Is an accounting necessary concerning classification of assets?
- ☐ Have you researched law supporting your theory?
- ☐ Will you want to present a trial memorandum on questions of classification?
- ☐ Do you need an accounting or tracing prepared?
- ☐ Will an expert be necessary/helpful regarding classification issues?

Business Valuation

- ☐ Do you have your business evaluation report?
- ☐ Have you produced your report?
- ☐ Are any updates necessary?
- ☐ Do you have the opposing expert report?
- ☐ Have you sent the opposing report to your expert?
- ☐ Are you going to depose the opposing expert?
- ☐ If you are deposing the expert, do you have a date set yet?
- ☐ Do you have time set aside to prepare for the deposition?
- ☐ Will your expert attend the opposing expert deposition? If so, do you have good dates for his or her availability?

Proving Income

- ☐ Do you have current income information?
- ☐ What is your theory regarding income?
- ☐ Are there any undisclosed cash issues?
- ☐ Do you have
  - ☐ current paystubs?
  - ☐ W-2s?
  - ☐ 1099s?
  - ☐ K-1s?
  - ☐ individual tax returns?
  - ☐ business tax returns?
  - ☐ bank statements?
  - ☐ credit card statements?

- ☐ Do you need an expert to support your theory of income?
- ☐ Is any forensic investigation or audit necessary to prove income?
- ☐ Will a lifestyle analysis help prove income?
- ☐ Do you have all necessary records to analyze family expenditures?
- ☐ Do you intend to use a summary?
  - ☐ Who will lay the foundation for the summary?
  - ☐ Have all data relied on in the summary been tendered to the opposing party?
  - ☐ Have you complied with all rules requiring service on summary exhibits on opposing counsel?

Taxes

- ☐ Are any tax issues in controversy?
- ☐ Have you calculated the tax impact of a particular property distribution?
- ☐ Do you need an accountant as a consulting or expert witness?
- ☐ Will the judge take judicial notice of a FinPlan or similar tax-calculation program?
- ☐ Have you solicited stipulations concerning tax calculations or the foundation of a tax report?

Child Custody

- ☐ Review all child custody reports/evaluations.
- ☐ Have you requested the underlying file/testing data of any adverse experts?
- ☐ Do you need an expert to deconstruct any adverse reports?
- ☐ Do you need a consulting expert as a trial consultant?
- ☐ Do you challenge the adverse expert based upon expertise or subject matter?
- ☐ Do you have the adverse expert's CV?
- ☐ Have you obtained any publications of adverse expert's?
- ☐ Should you depose any adverse experts?
- ☐ Assuming you decide to depose the adverse expert, has the date been set?
- ☐ Has time been set aside to prepare for the expert deposition?

- ☐ Who will be your witnesses?
- ☐ Will the children testify or be interviewed by the court?
- ☐ Is a motion necessary to permit the children to testify?
- ☐ Will a guardian ad litem or child representative be necessary?
- ☐ Have you disclosed all of your witnesses?
- ☐ Do you need to update your witness disclosures?
- ☐ Has the opposing party disclosed all witnesses?
- ☐ Has the opposing party's deposition been scheduled?
- ☐ Are any other depositions necessary or advisable?
- ☐ Review all correspondence and journals provided by client.

Evidentiary Planning

Relevance

- ☐ Is the evidence material and probative of an issue in controversy?
- ☐ Is the potential evidence cumulative?

Reliability aka Authentication

- ☐ Have you served a request to admit the genuineness of potential exhibits?
- ☐ Could you use the opposing party's deposition to seek an admission regarding authenticity?
- ☐ Did you receive the potential exhibit in response to a discovery request?
- ☐ If so, can you prove you received the particular document in discovery?
- ☐ Have you solicited a stipulation regarding authenticity and/or admission?
- ☐ Will the court take judicial notice of the authenticity of the exhibit?
- ☐ Is the exhibit self-authenticated under Rule 902(11)?
- ☐ Do you have all certificates to admit business records under Rule 902(11)?
- ☐ Is witness testimony based upon personal knowledge, memory, or sensory observations of the witness?

- ☐ Have you scripted the language to lay foundation through witness testimony?

Substantive Rules

- ☐ What possible objections might the opponent raise to the offer?
- ☐ Is the evidence an out-of-court statement?
- ☐ If it is an out-of-court statement, is it exempt from the hearsay rule as an admission of a party opponent?
- ☐ Is the statement being offered for some reason other than the truth of the matter asserted (notice, knowledge, etc.)?
- ☐ Do any exceptions apply to the out-of-court statement?
  - ☐ excited utterance
  - ☐ present sense impression
  - ☐ state of mind
  - ☐ past recollection recorded
  - ☐ records of regularly conducted activity (business records)
  - ☐ commercial publication
  - ☐ statement against interest
  - ☐ residual exception

60-Day Checklist

- ☐ Review your fee balance.
- ☐ Audit compliance with the fee agreement.
- ☐ Follow up with client if no compliance.
- ☐ Review all pleadings/orders.
- ☐ Do you need to amend or answer any pleadings?
- ☐ Prepare a docket book:
  - ☐ Compile all pleadings and orders.
  - ☐ Prepare docket book index.
- ☐ Do you have all transcripts?
- ☐ Have you abstracted all transcripts?
- ☐ Review and if necessary update the following:
  - ☐ proof chart
  - ☐ theory
  - ☐ theme
- ☐ Interview potential witnesses.
  - ☐ Consider the witnesses' demeanors.
  - ☐ Do the benefits of witnesses outweigh the risks of using them?
  - ☐ Is the witness cooperative?
  - ☐ If not cooperative, will the witness actively sabotage the case?
  - ☐ Is the witness available to testify?
- ☐ Is the witness subject to a subpoena/compulsory appearance?
- ☐ If the witness is out of state, do the costs of bringing in the witness warrant the price?
- ☐ Do the benefits of a deposition of an out-of-state witness warrant the costs of traveling to depose the witness?
- ☐ Is a video/closed-feed deposition an option?
- ☐ Can you use a deposition to authenticate potential exhibits?
- ☐ Should you depose any of your own witnesses if potentially unavailable at trial?
- ☐ Do you have any privilege issues to contend with?

- ☐ Do you need to obtain any releases or waivers for the testimony?
- ☐ Do you anticipate any Fifth Amendment issues for your witnesses?
- ☐ Do you expect any Fifth Amendment issues for opposing witnesses?
- ☐ Will you call any child witnesses?
- ☐ Will you have any competency issues?
- ☐ Will you be seeking an in camera interview with the children?
- ☐ Will the opposing party seek an in camera interview?
- ☐ Are any preliminary motions necessary regarding a child witness?
- ☐ Have you disclosed all of your witnesses?
- ☐ Have you received disclosures from the opposing party?
- ☐ Will you depose any adverse witnesses?
- ☐ Have you scheduled those depositions?
- ☐ Are all of your depositions complete?
- ☐ Have you analyzed whether to depose the opposing expert?
- ☐ If you are deposing the opposing expert, have you scheduled the deposition?
- ☐ Schedule time to prepare for the expert deposition.
- ☐ Can you informally interview any witnesses disclosed by the opposing party?
- ☐ Do you need to formally investigate any opposing-party witnesses?
- ☐ Have you discussed the adverse witnesses with your client?
- ☐ Have you sent written confirmation to your witnesses regarding the following?
    - ☐ date and time of the testimony
    - ☐ location
    - ☐ where and when to meet
    - ☐ prearranged date for preparation and rehearsal
    - ☐ general topic of testimony
    - ☐ instructions if contacted by opposing party, attorney, or investigator
    - ☐ explanation regarding subpoena

- ☐ Prepare subpoenas to the following:
  - ☐ ______________________________
  - ☐ ______________________________
  - ☐ ______________________________
- ☐ Are the subpoenas served?
  - ☐ Subpoena served on ______________________ this date ____________.
  - ☐ Subpoena served on ______________________ this date ____________.
  - ☐ Subpoena served on ______________________ this date ____________.

Witness Preparation

- ☐ Compile all documents related to witness testimony, including the following:
  - ☐ information sheet
  - ☐ copies of subpoenas
  - ☐ impeachment materials
  - ☐ witness outline
  - ☐ examination of each witness
- ☐ Prepare outline/structure of direct examination of all witnesses.
- ☐ Reduce outline to headnotes and proofs.
- ☐ Prepare cross-examination questions in rough draft.
- ☐ Rework cross-questions.

Exhibits

- ☐ Compile evidentiary exhibits.
- ☐ Pre-mark exhibits.
- ☐ Copy and bind exhibits.
- ☐ Prepare exhibit list.
- ☐ Prepare blank exhibit list for opposing-party exhibits.
- ☐ Authenticity established?
- ☐ Schedule exhibit conference with opposing counsel.

- ☐ Do you need to ask the court for exhibit conference?
- ☐ Would a demonstrative exhibit clarify witness testimony?
  - ☐ timelines
  - ☐ charts or graphs
  - ☐ blowups
  - ☐ poster boards
  - ☐ PowerPoint
  - ☐ whiteboard or flip chart
- ☐ Are you using any summaries?
- ☐ Have you provided all documents summarized?
  - ☐ Who will lay the foundation for the summary?

30-Day Checklist

- ☐ Prepare trial memorandum.
  - ☐ legal research
  - ☐ summary of the issues in dispute
  - ☐ summary of noncontroversial/undisputed facts
  - ☐ summary of witnesses disclosed by both parties
  - ☐ proposed exhibit list
  - ☐ any stipulations already reached or sought
- ☐ Prepare opening statement.
  - ☐ brainstorm grabber
  - ☐ outline
  - ☐ include references to theory and themes
  - ☐ rehearse
- ☐ Prepare closing argument.
  - ☐ written or oral?
  - ☐ include facts, law, and emotion
  - ☐ rehearse
- ☐ Will demonstrative aids help opening or closing?
  - ☐ how to use
  - ☐ when to use
  - ☐ formats (poster board, projection, PowerPoint, etc.)
  - ☐ prepare rough draft of demonstrative
  - ☐ finalize demonstrative aid
- ☐ Consider final pretrial motions.
  - ☐ motion in limine to bar cumulative testimony
  - ☐ motion to bar evidence or issues not properly disclosed
  - ☐ motion to pare down witness list
  - ☐ motion to have the admissibility of prospective evidence ruled on in advance
  - ☐ motion to determine anticipated claims of privilege
  - ☐ motion to take judicial notice of certain evidence

- ☐ motion for leave to call a witness out of order
- ☐ motion to bar witnesses from observing other witness testimony
- ☐ motion to allow an expert witness to observe opposing expert's testimony

☐ Prepare for final pretrial. Use the conference to do the following:

- ☐ solicit stipulations
- ☐ address evidentiary issues
- ☐ schedule witnesses

☐ Have exhibits been exchanged?

☐ Have you reviewed opposing party's proposed exhibits?

☐ Discuss with judge preferences with exhibits.

☐ Request necessary accommodations for client.

☐ Discuss settlement.

☐ Have all witnesses been confirmed?

☐ Are appointments set for preparation?

☐ Use client meeting to discuss the following:

- ☐ trial procedure
- ☐ format of testimony
- ☐ rules regarding objections
- ☐ possibility of being called as an adverse witness
- ☐ set up follow-up meeting with client to rehearse the direct examination

Other Witness Preparation

☐ Schedule preparation conferences.

☐ Discuss wardrobe and demeanor.

☐ Discuss trial procedure and protocol.

☐ Conduct a field trip to courthouse.

☐ Explain lawyer's role at trial.

☐ Confirm date, location, and time of testimony.

☐ Confirm where and who to meet at courthouse.

- ☐ Explain procedure and objections.
- ☐ Explain the role of the court reporter, bailiff, judge, etc.
- ☐ Order translator (if applicable).
- ☐ Provide rules of effective testimony.
    - ☐ speak loud and clear
    - ☐ moderate pace
    - ☐ listen, pause, and then answer
    - ☐ don't guess
    - ☐ what to do if you hear an objection
    - ☐ procedure for forgetfulness
- ☐ Discuss witnesses' direct examination.
    - ☐ overview of topics
    - ☐ procedure for foundations
    - ☐ rectifying mistakes
    - ☐ tell the truth
    - ☐ Fifth Amendment issues?
    - ☐ privilege issues
- ☐ Schedule a dress rehearsal for direct examination/cross-examination.
- ☐ Would a demonstrative aid enhance testimony?
    - ☐ If so, prepare the exhibit.
    - ☐ Explain how to use to client.
    - ☐ Format? (poster board, projector, whiteboard, etc.)
- ☐ Discuss expected cross-examination with the witness.
    - ☐ Answer only the question asked.
    - ☐ Don't argue.
    - ☐ Don't volunteer information.
    - ☐ Don't guess.
    - ☐ Think about the question.
    - ☐ The opposing lawyer is not your friend; don't agree to everything.
    - ☐ Correct mistakes.

- ☐ Cover likely topics.
- ☐ Any problems from the deposition to cure?
- ☐ Remember: you will have an opportunity to redirect witness.

☐ Conduct a dress rehearsal.

- ☐ Find associate or other lawyer to conduct.
- ☐ Deconstruct with witness.

☐ Prepare the expert.

- ☐ Discuss appropriate demeanor and tone.
- ☐ Get transcript from the deposition.
- ☐ Discuss problem areas.
- ☐ Make sure the CV is updated.
- ☐ Discuss how you will use demonstrative exhibits.
- ☐ Review the structure of your direct examination.
- ☐ Discuss how to handle himself or herself on cross.
- ☐ Discuss topics likely to be covered on cross.
- ☐ Discuss the procedure for hypotheticals.

7-Day Checklist

- ☐ Review your calendar.
  - ☐ Any conflicts?
  - ☐ Anything need to be rescheduled?
  - ☐ Have I set aside time after court to deconstruct the day?
  - ☐ Anything I should delegate?

Receivable Review

- ☐ Any settlement offers to review or discuss with your client?
- ☐ Coordinate the team.
  - ☐ Who will accompany you to trial?
  - ☐ Have you instructed that person?
  - ☐ Will someone set up and break down each day?
  - ☐ Will you use a technology assistant?
  - ☐ Can you get in early to set up?
  - ☐ Have you notified your assistant how to update you with daily developments?
  - ☐ Who will take your phone calls?
  - ☐ Set up an out-of-office e-mail assistant.
  - ☐ Who is lined up to handle emergencies?
  - ☐ Is someone available to make courthouse deliveries?

Miscellaneous Considerations

- ☐ How will you get to court?
- ☐ What time will you leave to go to court?
- ☐ Where will you have lunch?
- ☐ Will you need cash or change?
- ☐ Is your wardrobe determined?
- ☐ Personal grooming:
  - ☐ hair
  - ☐ nails
  - ☐ laundry or dry cleaning
  - ☐ shoeshine

- ☐ Practice opening and closing.
- ☐ Pack
  - ☐ trial notebook
  - ☐ copies of your exhibits with exhibit list
  - ☐ copies of opponent's exhibits with exhibit list
  - ☐ demonstrative exhibits with copy for court record
  - ☐ cell phone and power cord
  - ☐ laptop with power cord
  - ☐ electrical tape
  - ☐ projector
  - ☐ whiteboard
  - ☐ flip chart
  - ☐ markers
  - ☐ easels
  - ☐ extension cords
  - ☐ legal pads
  - ☐ index cards
  - ☐ sticky notes or flags
  - ☐ extra notepad for the client
  - ☐ pens and highlighters
  - ☐ paper clips or staplers
  - ☐ file folders
  - ☐ dictionary
  - ☐ evidence reference book
  - ☐ statute or code of procedure
  - ☐ personal items (glasses, lens cloth, hearing-aid battery)
  - ☐ water
  - ☐ energy drinks
  - ☐ energy snacks

- ☐ Download file to laptop.
- ☐ Check in with client.
- ☐ Prepare trial survival package.
- ☐ Double-check technology.
- ☐ Repeat positive affirmations.
- ☐ Relax!

Concluding the Case Checklist

- ☐ Review the ruling.
- ☐ Prepare a checklist with all follow-up tasks to complete:
  - ☐ Execute deeds.
  - ☐ Prepare title transfers or assignments: stock, vehicles, etc.
  - ☐ Do QDROs or transfer of retirement need to be done?
  - ☐ Any accounting necessary to implement judgment?
  - ☐ Deadlines for post-trial motions or appeal docketed?
  - ☐ Necessity of support withholding orders?
- ☐ Meet with the client to discuss the ruling:
  - ☐ advise of implications of ruling
  - ☐ next steps/options concerning post-trial motions or appeal
  - ☐ tax implications of ruling/divorce
  - ☐ changing estate plan
  - ☐ cancellation of joint debt
  - ☐ significant future dates
  - ☐ implications of noncompliance with court order
  - ☐ procedure for future modification (and what can be modified)
  - ☐ arrangements regarding outstanding fees
- ☐ Send letter to client confirming options and obligations.
- ☐ Throw a party for client?
- ☐ Purge the file.
  - ☐ Return originals to client.
  - ☐ Shred duplicates.
- ☐ Send thank-you notes/acknowledgments
- ☐ Keep a journal.

Bibliography

Boies, David. *Courting Justice: From NY Yankees v. Major League Baseball to Bush v. Gore, 1997-2000*. New York, NY: Hyperion, 2004. Print.

Buzan, Tony, and Barry Buzan. *The Mind Map Book: How to Use Radiant Thinking to Maximize Your Brain's Untapped Potential*. New York: Dutton, 1994. Print.

Cialdini, Robert B. *Influence: Science and Practice*. 4th ed. Boston, MA: Allyn and Bacon, 2001. Print.

Clark, Ronald H., George R. Dekle, and William S. Bailey. *Cross-examination Handbook: Persuasion, Strategies, and Techniques*. New York, NY: Aspen, 2011. Print.

Donovan, Karen. *V. Goliath: The Trials of David Boies*. New York: Pantheon, 2005. Print.

Foer, Joshua. *Moonwalking with Einstein: The Art and Science of Remembering Everything*. New York: Penguin, 2011. Print.

Garner, Bryan A. *The Winning Brief: 100 Tips for Persuasive Briefing in Trial and Appellate Courts*. New York: Oxford UP, 2004. Print.

Gold-Bikin, Lynne Z., and Stephen Kolodny. *The Divorce Trial Manual: From Initial Interview to Closing Argument*. Chicago, IL: Section of Family Law, American Bar Association, 2003. Print.

Guberman, Ross. *Point Made: How to Write like the Nation's Top Advocates*. Oxford: Oxford UP, 2011. Print.

Kocoras, Charles P. *May It Please the Court: A Story about One of America's Greatest Trial Lawyers*. Chicago, IL: Law Bulletin, 2015. Print.

Lubet, Steven. *Modern Trial Advocacy: Analysis and Practice*. Notre Dame, IN: National Institute for Trial Advocacy, 1997. Print.

Lucas, Richard H., and K. Byron McCoy. *The Winning Edge: Effective Communication and Persuasion Techniques for Lawyers*. New York: Wiley Law Publications, 1993. Print.

McCormick, Charles, and Kenneth S. Broun. *McCormick on Evidence*. St. Paul, MN: Thomson/West, 2006. Print.

McElhaney, James W. *McElhaney's Trial Notebook*. 3rd ed. Chicago, IL: American Bar Association, 1994. Print.

Meyer, Philip N. *Storytelling for Lawyers*. New York: Oxford UP, 2014. Print.

Molo, Steven F., and James R. Figliulo. *Your Witness: Lessons on Cross-examination and Life from Great Chicago Trial Lawyers*. Chicago, IL: Law Bulletin, 2008. Print.

Nizer, Louis. *Reflections without Mirrors an Autobiography of the Mind*. Garden City, NY: Doubleday, 1978. Print.

Peskind, Steven N. *Family Law Trial Evidence Handbook: Rules and Procedures for Effective Advocacy*. Chicago, IL: American Bar Association, 2013. Print.

Rossman, George. *Classic Essays on Legal Advocacy*. Clark, NJ: Lawbook Exchange, 2010. Print.

Scalia, Antonin, and Bryan A. Garner. *Making Your Case: The Art of Persuading Judges*. St. Paul, MN: Thomson/West, 2008. Print.

Small, Daniel I. *Preparing Witnesses: A Practical Guide for Lawyers and Their Clients*. 4th ed. Chicago, IL: ABA, 2014. Print.

Spence, Gerry. *How to Argue and Win Every Time: At Home, at Work, in Court, Everywhere, Every Day*. New York: St. Martin's, 1995. Print.

Spence, Gerry. *Win Your Case*. New York: St. Martin's, 2005. Print.

Stryker, Lloyd Paul. *The Art of Advocacy: A Plea for the Renaissance of the Trial Lawyer*. New York: Simon and Schuster, 1954. Print.

Tigar, Michael E. *Examining Witnesses*. Chicago, IL: Section of Litigation, American Bar Association, 1993. Print.

Tigar, Michael E. *Persuasion: The Litigator's Art*. Chicago, IL: Section of Litigation, American Bar Association, 1999. Print.

Waicukauski, Ronald J., Paul Mark Sandler, and JoAnne A. Epps. *The Winning Argument*. Chicago, IL: Section of Litigation, American Bar Association, 2001. Print.

Wellman, Francis L. *The Art of Cross-examination: With the Cross-examinations of Important Witnesses in Some Celebrated Cases*. New York: Dorset, 1986. Print.

Worden, John S. *From the Trenches: Strategies and Tips from 21 of the Nation's Top Trial Lawyers*. Chicago, IL: ABA, 2015. Print.

Index